THE FOOD OF
INDONESIA

Authentic Recipes from the Spice Islands

Recipes by *Heinz von Holzen* & *Lother Arsana*

Food photography by *Heinz von Holzen*

Introduction and editing by *Wendy Hutton*

Produced in association with the Grand Hyatt Bali

PERIPLUS
EDITIONS

Contents

Part One: Food in Indonesia

A cuisine as exciting and diverse as the country itself

Indonesia is the world's largest archipelago, literally thousands of islands ranging from those among the world's largest to tiny coral atolls marooned in a sapphire sea. With terrain including snow-capped mountains and lush rainforests, arid savannah, swamps and irrigated rice fields, it's hard to imagine a more appropriate national motto than *Bhinneka Tunggal Ika*—Unity in Diversity.

Over the past two thousand years, powerful Buddhist, Hindu and Muslim kingdoms rose and fell in Sumatra, Java and Borneo, attracting merchants from China, the Middle East and India, as well as nearby Siam and Malacca. Some of the archipelago's eastern isles were the original Spice Islands, the only place in the world where cloves and nutmeg grew, a powerful magnet for the ever-expanding Europeans.

As ships set forth on voyages of discovery during the 16th and 17th centuries, the Portuguese, Spanish, English and Dutch began to arrive in the archipelago. The Dutch were the final victors in the battle for control over the region, introducing a plantation system to the colony, where laborers toiled to produce sugar, spices, rubber, tea and coffee (the original "cup of Java"). A nationalist movement was founded as early as 1908, but it was not until 1949 that the Republic of Indonesia came into being, after an armed struggle against the Dutch following Indonesia's declaration of independence in 1945.

With its enormous geographic and cultural diversity, it is not surprising that the cuisines of Indonesia are so varied. However, as restaurants in both Indonesia and abroad tend to focus on the food of Java and Sumatra, many non-Indonesians are unaware that each region has its own distinct cuisine. These indigenous styles have been influenced to varying degrees over the centuries by the introduction of ingredients and cooking styles from China, India, the Middle East and Europe.

The "typical" Indonesian meal might be described as being based on rice, with several savory side dishes of vegetable, fish or perhaps some meat or poultry, accompanied by a chili-hot condiment or *sambal*, with peanuts, wafers (*krupuk*) or fried shallots to provide a crunchy contrast. While such a description might be valid for much of Java, Sumatra and Bali, in other areas of the archipelago, the staple might be sago, cassava or corn.

Increasing numbers of visitors are discovering the rich cultural diversity of Indonesia, venturing off the beaten Bali-Java-Sumatra tourist track. Let us take you on a voyage of culinary discovery, exploring the unknown and revealing more about the already familiar.

Page 2:
Wrapped up in an ikat *cloth against the chill of dawn, this man gives a warm smile typical of Indonesians.*
Opposite:
Rice (top left) is the basis of every main meal, with side dishes of meat, poultry, fish or vegetables plus crunchy garnishes and sambals *(top right & center).*

Tanah Air: Land and Water

An archipelago of snow-capped mountains, rainforest, rice fields, swamps and savannah

Millions of acres of irrigated rice fields produce not only the staff of life but eels, small fish, food for the ducks and a pleasant place for cattle to cool down.

Stretching 5,000 miles from the northwest tip of Sumatra to the swamps of southwest Irian Jaya, Indonesia's 18,000 or so islands (home to some 190 million people) range from roughly 6 degrees north of the equator to 11 degrees south. The large islands of Sumatra, Java, Borneo (where two-thirds of the land mass is occupied by Indonesian Kalimantan) and Bali were part of the Asian mainland until permanently isolated by the end of the last Ice Age.

Indonesia is within the so-called "Ring of Fire," the meeting point of two of the earth's tectonic plates, which gives rise to frequent seismic activity. Smoldering volcanoes—like the Hindu god, Shiva, both Creator and Destroyer—periodically shower fertile ash on the land.

To a large extent, the western islands of Indonesia are lush and evergreen. While Borneo has rainforests and swampy coastlines, Java and Sumatra abound with fertile gardens, coconut groves and paddy fields. Fast-flowing rivers and glorious beaches complete the picture of a tropical paradise.

All of Indonesia enjoys tropical warmth and relatively high humidity (although the temperature drops significantly on the mountains), and most parts of the archipelago experience a definite dry season followed by life-giving monsoon rains. However, the eastern islands of the archipelago (especially Nusa Tenggara, the chain of islands from Lombok east to Timor) are often rocky and semi-arid, the dry seasons longer and harsher, and the land often degraded by tree felling and subsequent erosion.

Sulawesi (the Celebes), a strangely shaped island that was created when two islands slowly collided several million years ago, has a variety of climates and different parts receive their monsoon rains at different times of year. Farther east, the Spice Islands of Maluku (the Moluccas) once again obligingly conform to the image of the lush tropics, while Irian Jaya (the western portion of the huge island of New Guinea) has everything from swamps to rainforest to the highest mountain east of the Himalayas, the 16,000-foot snow-capped Mount Jaya.

The preferred staple throughout Indonesia is rice, which is grown both in irrigated paddies (where up to three crops a year can be achieved by using special strains of rice and fertilizers) and in non-irrigated fields, which depend on the monsoon rains. In many areas of the archipelago, however, either insufficient rainfall or unsuitable terrain make rice-growing impossible, and crops such as sweet potato, tapioca (also known as cassava or manioc), corn and which is often simply fried with a little seasoning of sour tamarind, turmeric and salt, or simmered in seasoned water or coconut milk. There are, of course, hundreds of more complex recipes for both freshwater fish (often raised in ponds) as well as sea fish. Because of limited transport and refrigeration, however, dried fish is more commonly encountered than fresh in many areas. Tiny dried anchovy-like fish known as *ikan teri* give flavor as well as protein

even sago are the staple. Those who can afford it will buy rice imported from other regions of Indonesia, but in very remote or subsistence areas, the traditional staple still reigns supreme. As an economy measure, Indonesians sometimes add corn or sweet potato to their daily rice to give extra substance; this also has the bonus of varying the flavor.

Not surprisingly for an archipelago, the most popular accompaniment to the staple food is fish, to a number of savory snacks and spicy or crunchy *sambals*.

Although vegetables are grown throughout Indonesia, they do not figure prominently in the diet in many areas. Certain wild leaves and plants, as well as the young leaves of plants grown for their fruit or tubers (such as starfruit, papaya, sweet potatoes and tapioca) are cooked as a vegetable. These are supplemented with a few easily grown veg-

islands, have borrowed ingredients and cooking styles from many sources over the centuries. Arab and Indian traders brought their spices, sweet rose essence and one or two popular dishes (including Indian Martabak, a type of pancake found at thousands of food stalls).

The Spanish were responsible for the introduction of chilies, which they discovered in the New World and carried to the islands of the Philippines. These fiery fruits swept throughout Southeast Asia and India and are so firmly established as part of the local cuisines that it's hard to imagine the food without them.

Despite their long period as colonial rulers, the Dutch, apart from the introduction of new vegetables and bread, did not have an enormous impact on the local cuisines. A word here about the so-called "Indonesian" *rijstaffel*. This was a colonial invention, a larger-than-life adaptation of the Indonesian style of serving rice with several savory side dishes and condiments. With time, money and plenty of servants to make almost anything possible, the Dutch developed a "rice table" where as many as 18–20 dishes might be served, each borne into the dining room by a comely maiden or uniformed "boy."

It is the Chinese who have had the greatest influence on the food of Indonesia. They introduced the now ubiquitous noodles (*mie*); soy sauce, which the Indonesians modified to suit their taste by adding sugar (*kecap manis*); mung peas used to make bean sprouts (*taugeh*); bean curd and soy beans, which the Indonesians learned how to ferment to make the excellent and nutritious *tempeh*.

etables, such as water spinach (*kangkung*), long beans, eggplant, pumpkins and cucumbers. Elevated areas, especially in islands with rich volcanic soil, have proved perfect for temperate climate vegetables. The Dutch introduced carrots, potatoes, cauliflower, cabbage and tomatoes, enthusiastically adopted by Indonesians with access to well-stocked markets.

Indonesia's cuisines, especially in the major

Eating Across the Archipelago

*A food lover's travels
from Irian Jaya to Sumatra*

What do a feast of pig steamed over hot stones in an earth oven, a ritual *selamatan* centered upon a golden rice mountain blessed by Muslim prayers, a bamboo tube of buffalo meat spiked with incendiary chilies roasted over a fire and satay of minced seafood mixed with spices and fresh coconut have in common?

A warm welcome awaits visitors throughout the archipelago, especially in small villages.

They're just some of the foods I have enjoyed in travels throughout Indonesia over more than two decades. Visitors encountering the same limited noodle and *nasi goreng* dishes in restaurants or *rumah makan* might be forgiven for thinking that there's more unity than diversity in the food of the archipelago. It's only if you brave the locally owned *warung* or simple food stalls (as opposed to those run by Javanese migrants offering the ubiquitous Soto Madura and Mie Bakso), if you arrive when a festival is going on or, best of all, are able to stay in Indonesian homes, that you have a chance of discovering the diversity of Indonesia's cuisines.

Some 3,200 feet up in the highlands of Irian Jaya, in western New Guinea, lies a fertile, stream-slashed valley isolated from the world by almost impenetrable swamps and jungle-covered mountains. The Baliem Valley, found by explorers traveling by seaplane in 1938 and visited by its first anthropologists only in 1961, is the home of the stone-age Dani people. They are skilled gardeners growing a variety of vegetables, yet 90 percent of their diet is made up of sweet potato. Although some seventy varieties are grown, after several days of eating this admirable tuber for breakfast, lunch and dinner, an outsider finds they all begin to taste identical.

While trekking in this beautiful wild valley in 1976, we passed a hamlet where great activity was going on. Like all Indonesians, the Dani are both hospitable and friendly and literally dragged me and my two young children into the compound to join what proved to be a wedding feast. The men, splendid in penis gourds, faces painted with colored clay and feathers stuck in their woolly black hair, lounged about playing bamboo mouth harps. The women, naked but for a string skirt perched precariously low on their hips, were almost knee-deep in freshly slaughtered pig, busy wrapping chunks of meat in leaves and stacking them onto river stones heated by a fire. Mounds of the inevitable sweet potato were laid on top of the pork, followed by a huge pile of leaves. The whole lot was then left to steam—just like a Maori *hangi* which, as a child, I had regarded as unique to New Zealand.

The food was eventually pronounced cooked and a leaf bundle of pork handed to me by an incredibly filthy woman. As I sat staring at the steaming pork, I thought of all the diseases I might catch. Sheer hunger and desperation for something other than sweet potato finally won out. Unwrapping my little packet of salt (a precious item in the valley where it could be traded for other goods), I sprinkled the pork and took my first mouthful. Moist, sweet, full of flavor—I will never forget my Dani pig feast! Even the sweet potatoes tasted good steamed in this earth oven (and I suffered no after-effects whatsoever).

By contrast, the central Javanese city of Yogyakarta seems to be located on an entirely different planet. Ancient stone temples—including the world-famous Buddhist Borobudur monument and the exquisite spires of Hindu Prambanan—rise up from the surrounding rice fields, while the classic cone of Mount Merapi periodically showers the land with rich volcanic ash.

The Javanese of the sultanates of Yogyakarta and nearby Surakarta are proud of their refined culture, their dances, *gamelan* music, *batik* fabric and intricate handicrafts. Theirs is a highly structured society where harmony depends upon consideration for others, the group being more important than the individual. Ritual events are marked by a communal feast (*selamatan*), so it was appropriate that our arrival in the household of a Yogya family, where we were to stay for a year, was the occasion for such a feast.

Prayers were said to confer blessings upon our family and everyone present. The centerpiece of the *selamatan* was a cone-shaped mound of yellow rice, symbolic of the metaphysical Hindu Mount Meru. (Although most Javanese are Muslim, earlier animistic, Buddhist and Hindu observances are still incorporated in their rituals.) At least a dozen dishes accompanied the rice, including *gudeg* (young jackfruit cooked in coconut milk); fried chicken, which had first been simmered in spiced coconut milk; fermented soy bean cakes (*tempeh*) fried with shrimp

Local markets, such as this one in Banjarmasin, Southern Kalimantan, are invariably full of color.

and sweetened with palm sugar; red chili *sambal* and crisp shrimp wafers (*krupuk*). The overall impression was one of subtlety and sweetness, a harmonious blend quintessentially Javanese.

There's nothing subtle, however, about the food of the west Sumatran region of Padang. If you like it hot and spicy (and thousands of Indonesians do, for Padang restaurants are found in most cities throughout the country), you'll have no hesitation in calling this some of the best food in Indonesia. In a nation full of stunning scenery, the rugged mountains, lakes and glorious coastline of west Sumatra more than hold their own. The ridiculously picturesque town of Bukittinggi ("High Hill"), the heartland of the matriarchal Minang people, is perfect for sampling the local food.

This is one of the few cuisines best enjoyed in a restaurant or simple eating shop, since it is the spicy counterpart of a smorgasbord. Portions taken from ten to as many as twenty different dishes are carried from their display counter and placed on the restaurant table. You help yourself to whatever you wish to eat, paying only for what you consume. You don't fancy brains in a rich, spicy coconut-milk sauce? Never mind, try chicken in coconut milk fragrant with lemongrass, black slices of beef

dendeng, chicken livers with bitter green beans (*petai*), large prawns coated with pounded chili, eggs in spicy sauce—the list literally goes on and on.

Most people would describe Padang food as spicy, but dried spices are only part of the story. Look into the hilltop market of Bukittinggi, where the proud Minang women are resplendent in bright colors and even the bird cages are clothed in vivid velvet. There are mounds of cinnamon, pepper, coriander, chili powder, cumin and fennel, yet just as vital to Padang food are the herbs, rhizomes and other seasonings.

These include chilies, ginger, garlic, shallots, galangal, turmeric, lemongrass, basil, fragrant lime and *salam* leaves and pungent dried shrimp paste. Nearby lie piles of ripe brown coconuts, their flesh destined to make the rich, creamy milk that soothes (if only slightly) the impact of much Padang food, which is always served with steaming white rice to counterbalance the emphatic flavors.

Rice was, however, nowhere evident when we spent a night in what we nicknamed "The House of Sago" in the tiny island of Saparua. We had sailed there from Ambon, in the heart of the original Spice Islands, in search of an ancient Dutch fort that once helped protect the lucrative spice trade. As Saparua

was, in those days, too undeveloped for even the most simple *losmen* or lodging house, we went armed with an introduction to Oma Lela, the grandmother of a friend in Ambon.

Her dirt-floored house was roofed in sago palm fronds, the walls made of stout palm ribs, the roll-up blinds outside the open windows cut from split palm ribs. With the overwhelming hospitality we encountered countless times in Indonesia, she gave us her bedroom; the bedside table was covered with a cloth she had embroidered, and a simple plastic comb, a jar of hair pomade and a box of mosquito coils put out for our comfort.

We had already sampled a form of sago near Ambon, where *popeda*—a mass of tasteless gluey starch made from the grated and pounded sago palm trunk—is the traditional staple food. Oma Lela, however, used squares of dried sago "bread" made by baking the gluey starch in terra-cotta molds.

The hard pinkish cakes were considered by 19th-century naturalist Alfred Russel Wallace to be "quite a delicacy when made with the addition of a little sugar and grated cocoa-nut." He also noted that people dependent upon sago eat very little vegetables or fruit, living "almost entirely on sago and fish." This was exactly our meal at Oma's house, where the sago bread was soaked in water to reconstitute it before frying. To accompany it, little fish flavored with dried turmeric and salt were also crisp fried, the resulting meal all the more satisfying because of the generosity with which it was prepared.

With its thousands of miles of coastline, the orchid-shaped island of Sulawesi (Celebes) is renowned for its fish. *Ikan bakar*, fish roasted over charcoal and served with a variety of dipping sauces, is a firm regional favorite, yet one of my most memorable meals in Sulawesi was enjoyed in the highlands of Tana Toraja. The scenery of mountains with villages marooned like islands in a sea of paddy fields is more than enough to attract visitors, yet an additional lure is the unique architecture and culture of the mostly Christian people of Tana Toraja.

Anxious to see their cliff burial sites with hanging balconies peopled by wooden statues of the departed, I spent almost an entire evening bumping by bus from Ujung Pandang to Rantepao. Awaking after a couple of hours' sleep, I noticed a stream of people on the road in front of my *losmen*. They were heading for a funeral, the most important event in the Torajan life cycle and an occasion for ritual feasting.

Not long afterwards, I was seated in one of the

Vegetables introduced by the Dutch and now widely popular are grown at higher altitudes, especially in Sumatra (these girls are in the town of Brastagi), Java, Bali and Sulawesi.

leaves and a few fiery bird's-eye chilies. The bamboo tubes were stoppered with banana leaf and roasted over an open fire. Eaten with excellent hill rice and washed down with *tuak*, this was indeed a memorable feast.

Feasts are commonplace in Bali, and I have spent many happy hours helping to chop and pound seasonings, slicing boiled pig's ear for the ceremonial *lawar*, coloring rice cakes and composing ritual temple offerings. Yet even relatively simple food in Bali can be excellent. Other Indonesians may sniff that the Balinese "pad out" their satay by adding coconut flesh rather than using pure meat or chicken, yet Sate Lilit, made of highly seasoned chopped seafood or poultry mixed with coconut and molded around a stalk of fragrant lemongrass is the best satay I've sampled in the entire archipelago.

The interior highlands of the so-called wilds of Borneo bring back wonderful memories of wild boar caught in the surrounding rainforest and smoked over a fire, of tender, sweet bamboo shoots thrusting up through the soil, of wild ferns that rival asparagus for flavor.

Travel in Indonesia always means food, not just at the destination but en route, too. Buses stop at 2 AM so that passengers can buy from the villagers who sell, in the light of their flickering kerosene lamps, the delicacy for which they are renowned. Passengers on board ship share their home-prepared boneless stuffed fish or sticky rice rolls enclosing savory stuffings. Endless islands, endless variety, endless generosity. One could go on eating across Indonesia forever.

bamboo shelters built to house guests during the lengthy funeral celebrations. Streams of men staggered up the slippery hillside bearing stout bamboos filled with frothing local palm wine (*tuak*) and with pigs strung by their feet from bamboo poles. The inevitable and somewhat gruesome slaughter of pigs and water buffalo was followed by the preparation of *piong*, bamboo tubes stuffed with chunks of lightly salted meat, fresh blood, spinach

Islands That Changed the World

The rich treasures of Indonesia's Spice Islands prompted the Age of Exploration

Apart from the crumbling remains of Portuguese and Dutch forts, there's little that sets several small Moluccan islands apart from countless other islands in Indonesia. Yet five of these islands were once the only place in the world where cloves grew, while another group, the Bandas, were the sole source of nutmeg and mace. These islands were literally responsible for starting the Age of Exploration and for the discovery of the Americas by Christopher Columbus.

With today's refrigeration and food processing, it's hard to fully appreciate the importance of spices in ancient times. Cloves, pepper and nutmeg were sought by the Romans, Egyptians and Chinese as long as two thousand years ago, used in cooking to add flavor and to help mask the flavors of less-than-fresh meat, to perfume the air during funerals and to sweeten the mouth. They were also used in medicines and magical potions.

During the Middle Ages, the spice trade in Europe was controlled by Arab merchants, who in turn bought from Indian traders. They kept prices astronomically high by supplying Venetian merchants, who then distributed the goods to the rest of Europe. The search for the source of these spices caused Christopher Columbus to stumble upon the Americas (he thought he was going to reach India). Other voyages of exploration were made by the Portuguese, who eventually reached the Spice Islands of Maluku (Moluccas) by the beginning of the 16th century, followed not long after by the Spanish, English and Dutch.

In 1602 the Dutch set up the East Indies Company to exploit the riches of the archipelago that was eventually to become Indonesia. They ruthlessly achieved a total monopoly of the spice trade by the end of the 17th century, and any grower who traded illegally was punished by having his clove trees cut down. By the 19th century, however, clove seedlings smuggled out of the Spice Islands eventually ended the worldwide monopoly once enjoyed by the Dutch.

Ironically, more cloves are now grown in northern Sulawesi than in Maluku, and Indonesia imports

The nutmeg fruit consists of an edible fleshy outer portion; inside, the hard brown seed or nutmeg is covered with a lacy red aril known as mace. Nutmeg once grew only on the Banda islands, in Maluku.

Boats fashioned entirely from cloves (the dried bud of a tree native to just five islands in Maluku) are a popular souvenir item today in the Spice Islands. The majority of Indonesia's clove crop today goes up in smoke in the form of clove-scented cigarettes.

mats of drying cloves are still a common sight in Maluku. Picked green, the fragrant nail-shaped flower bud of the *Eugenia aromatica* is sun dried for several days, turning beige and finally the familiar rich dark brown of the cloves found on supermarket shelves around the world. Tall nutmeg trees, regarded by many as the most beautiful of cultivated trees, still thrive on the islands of Banda and, to a lesser extent, on Ambon. The ripe fruit is picked and the hard fragrant nut extracted; often the nimble fingers of children are employed to separate the bright scarlet aril or mace from the nut, which is then dried.

Cloves and nutmeg are, perhaps surprisingly, rarely used in cooking in the Moluccas. Although a little grated nutmeg may be added to a rich beef soup, nutmeg and cloves are regarded more as medicinal plants. Nutmeg fruit, the fleshy covering of the hard nut which is used as a spice, is usually pickled and eaten as a snack. It is also the traveler's friend, considered good for seasickness, while cloves are the universal cure for toothache.

cloves from Tanzania to meet the demand for the spice. Don't expect to find it in many Indonesian dishes, however—most of the cloves literally go up in smoke, added to tobacco for the distinctive *keretek* cigarettes. Nutmeg has lost much of its value and demand is now considerably less than supply.

Despite the drop in value of these spices (which could realize a profit of 1,000 percent for early explorers who returned with a full cargo hold), woven

While these are indigenous spices, some of the

other spices used in Indonesian cooking came from the Middle East or India, such as cardamom, fibrous pods containing tiny black seeds known in the Middle Ages as "grains of paradise," native to India and Sri Lanka. True cinnamon grows in Sri Lanka, while the coarse bark sold as cinnamon in Indonesia and other parts of Southeast Asia comes from a type of cassia tree. Coarser, darker in color and less expensive, it adds a robust flavor to some meat dishes.

The most widely used spice in Indonesia is coriander, a small round beige seed with a faintly orange flavor. This spice was known to the ancient Greeks and is found throughout the Middle East and India, as well as in Southeast Asia. Coriander is commonly partnered with peppercorns and garlic to flavor food, especially in Java.

Another spice often used in conjunction with coriander is cumin, an elongated seed that looks and even smells a little like caraway. A similar spice, fennel, is fatter, whiter and sweeter in fragrance than cumin.

Both black and white peppercorns, each of which has its distinct flavor, are used in most parts of the archipelago. Peppercorns are the berry of a vine native to the Malabar coast of India, brought to Indonesia many centuries ago. Black peppercorns are the dried ripe berry with the skin intact, while white peppercorns have had the skins removed.

Coastal areas of Indonesia, which were major trading centers (such as the eastern seaboard of Sumatra and which saw Arab and India traders long before the Chinese and Europeans arrived, and the west and north coasts of Java), use a wider range

Left:
Chilies, brought to Asia from the Americas by the Portuguese four centuries ago, are an indispensable ingredient in Indonesian cuisine, whether whole or ground into a fiery paste.
Overleaf:
Fishing in Indonesia's warm clear waters is a pleasure rather than a chore for these boys.

of spices and seasonings than areas that had little contact with the outside world. While some Sumatran dishes, for example, may call for as many as six or seven different spices and at least as many other roots, herbs and seasonings, a dish from a remote island in eastern Indonesia may be flavored with turmeric and salt only, or cooked without seasoning and eaten with a dipping sauce or spicy *sambal*.

An Invitation to the Feast

How an Indonesian
meal is composed and eaten

"*S ilahkan makan*" is the polite Indonesian invitation that proceeds any meal served to guests (and a phrase foreigners should always wait for before beginning even as much as a snack served by their Indonesian hosts).

But in countless homes throughout the archipelago, meals are usually an informal affair and often eaten alone. Millions of Indonesian women are up before dawn, and the fragrance of wood cooking fires weaves through the freshness of the early morning on their return from market with the day's provisions. Before the task of cooking begins, there will be a simple breakfast, often some leftover food from the night before, perhaps a few sticky cakes from the market, a bowl of noodles or simple fried rice.

Meals may be communal affairs, as is this lunch in a Borneo logging camp, although it's just as likely for family members to eat alone.

The most popular staple food is rice (although there are variations in many regions) and Indonesians eat surprisingly large amounts of it, together with a number of savory side dishes and condiments. Only small amounts of these savory dishes —which may include fish, poultry, meat, eggs, vegetables, bean curd or *tempeh*—are eaten. Variety rather than volume is the name of the game, Indonesians preferring to enjoy just a little of four or five side dishes rather than large helpings of only one or two.

Condiments are just as important as the savory dishes and will usually include a chili-hot *sambal* as well as something to provide a crunchy contrast. This could be deep-fried *tempeh*, peanuts, deep-fried tiny anchovies (*ikan teri*), *krupuk* (wafers made of tapioca flour seasoned with anything from fish to prawns to bitter *melinjo* nuts), a seasoned fried coconut concoction such as *serundeng* or fried peanut wafers (*rempeyek*).

The rice and accompanying dishes are normally cooked early in the day, immediately after a trip to the market or using food gathered from the garden. Many meals, especially in the more remote areas of this far-flung archipelago, are extremely simple and may consist of the local staple plus items such as a little dried fish, chili *sambal* with, perhaps, some deep-fried shallots or a *sambal* of sweet soy sauce with some chopped herbs or a squeeze of citrus juice.

The prepared food is usually set in a cupboard or on a table in the kitchen, protected from insects by conical food covers made of woven pandanus leaf or plastic. Members of the family help themselves to whatever they want whenever hungry, or some may take a container of food to the fields to be eaten at midday. Evening meals, taken at the end of the day when family members return from the fields, from school or their work in the towns and cities, are often based on food leftover from the main midday meal, with one or two extra dishes cooked if necessary.

As the food is often eaten some time after it has been prepared, it is usually at room temperature (no one will waste expensive fuel reheating it). Modern Indonesian homes in the towns and cities often have rice cookers, which keep cooked rice warm for several hours, but most Indonesians are unconcerned if the rice is not hot.

Where meals are communal, the rice and all the accompanying dishes are placed in the middle of the table or on a mat on the floor at the one time, and everyone helps themselves to whatever they want. It is considered impolite to pile one's plate with food at the first serving; just a little will do, as there's plenty of opportunity to take more food as the meal progresses.

Indonesians traditionally eat with the right hand (the left is considered unclean by Muslims), although serving spoons are used to transfer the food to individual plates or bowls from the serving dishes. Many modern homes and almost all restaurants provide a spoon and fork, while chopsticks can be expected in Chinese restaurants.

In more affluent homes, the choice of dishes to accompany the rice is made with a view to achieving a blend of flavors and textures. If one of the savory dishes has a rich, coconut-milk gravy, this will be offset by a dry dish with perhaps a sharper flavor. There may well be a pungent *sambal goreng* (food fried with a spicy chili seasoning), but this will be balanced with other mild or even sweet dishes using *kecap manis* (sweet black soy sauce) or palm sugar.

Part of the joy of cooking Indonesian food is planning the range of dishes. As so many of them can be prepared well in advance, a multi-course meal for family or friends, even in the West, does not require lonely hours in the kitchen as others relax and await the feast.

Gorgeously dressed Buginese girls in Southern Sulawesi enjoy a meal where, in typical Indonesian style, rice and accompanying dishes are placed in the center of the table for everyone to help themselves.

Eating Out

From the local warung food stall to moveable meals on wheels and tasty snacks

The English have their pubs, the French their cafes, but in Indonesia, it is the *warung* that is the social center of most villages and small towns. Usually made of either woven bamboo or wood, open-fronted with dirt or cement floors, the *warung* is the Indonesian equivalent of the corner mom and pop store, offering everything you might need in a hurry (mosquito coils, laundry soap, matches, clove-scented cigarettes).

Warung also sell a bewildering and colorful array of packaged snacks, cakes, cookies, bottles of drink and maybe even an enamel plate piled high with fresh bananas, avocados, papayas or guavas gathered from a nearby garden.

The *warung* is where women stop for a chat on their way back from the market; where children buy a packet of crisp *krupuk* wafers to munch on en route for school; where those who want something refreshing might order a freshly made *rujak*, a combination of crisp, sour fruit and vegetables slathered in a pungent, chili-hot sauce, and where

Whenever the need for a snack strikes (and it often does in Indonesia) a warung *offers plenty of options, such as the giant* krupuk *(prawn cracker) these boys are sharing.*

the men pause for a coffee or an early evening glass of *tuak* (palm wine). After night has fallen, young men dream their dreams together under the flickering oil lamp until the *warung* owner finally packs up for the day. *Warung*, which are usually locally owned, frequently offer a couple of simple dishes and are excellent places for the visitor to sample the local cuisine.

It may be difficult to discover that fresh food is actually on sale at a *warung*, as the competition from other goods is almost overwhelming. The large granite grinding stone used to make the spicy dressing for *rujak* is often tucked away behind the counter, and the same may be true for leaf-wrapped bundles of food.

Eating out for many Indonesians is usually a necessity rather than a luxury, and basic food stalls selling cooked food at very reasonable prices are found in any large village as well as in towns and cities. Food stalls cluster along back lanes or spring up around markets on market day. Other stalls mushroom at night, with a table, a couple of benches and a plastic roof set up in the market square at dusk.

Gas fires roar and oil sizzles as bananas are dipped in batter and deep fried, or rice or noodles are flipped around a wok at amazing speed. The smell of charcoal permeates the air as the inevitable satay is grilled, while large flat pancakes are slapped on a griddle and spread with a savory meat mixture for the popular Indian Muslim snack, Martabak.

Stalls are often a good source of regional favorites. You will, for example, find Soto Makassar (a rich beef soup) and grilled fish (Ikan Bakar) along Ujung Pandang's waterfront in Southern Sulawesi. Lombok's favorite chicken, which is grilled over coals and served with a spicy sauce (Ayam Taliwang) is found at many food stalls in the capital, Mataram, and almost any market in Bali will feature the famous roast pig (Babi Guling).

Market food stalls often sell a plate of rice with small portions of several "dishes of the day"; Nasi Campur (literally "mixed rice") is economical and the various vegetables, meat, poultry or fish dishes accompanying the rice are often cooked in the regional style.

It is, however, sometimes surprisingly difficult for travelers to find genuine local food. This situation came about as thousands of Javanese leave their overcrowded homeland every year and settle— often as part of the official government resettlement or *transmigrasi* scheme—everywhere from Irian Jaya to Borneo. As is the case the world over, migrants often make a living by selling food. Hence, the Javanese "culinary imperialism," which guarantees you'll find Soto Ayam, Sate Madura and Mie Bakso almost anywhere you find a food stall.

Itinerant hawkers also tend to be Javanese. The resonant "tock tock" of two lengths of bamboo being struck or the metallic twang of a type of clapper are often heard together with the voice of the hawker calling out his wares. Many families buy noodle soup, rolled pancakes with a fresh coconut and palm sugar filling or sticky rice cakes (*jaja*) for their breakfast from these hawkers. Throughout the day, there's a steady procession of rumbling pushcarts, makeshift wooden contraptions resting on a couple of bicycle wheels, offering Mie Bakso (noodle and meat ball soup), or bowls of shaved ice with the syrups, jellies and fruits of your choice added. Another hawker with a charcoal fire pauses to grill satay on request.

It's enough to make one wonder why anyone bothers cooking at home.

Mobile carts or food stalls set up outside a market or along a road generally offer Javanese favorites. Regional dishes, however, can also be found in such places, if you know where to look.

Fantastic Thirst Quenchers

You can have your drink and eat it, too

Like a child's fantasy on the loose, many of Indonesia's drinks are a riot of colors, flavors and textures, concoctions so chock-full of goodies that you're not sure whether you're supposed to eat them or drink them. (In fact, you often do both.)

Throughout the land there are hawkers carrying a couple of large baskets on either end of a bamboo pole, mobile pushcarts and market stalls, all dispensing drinks that are both thirst-quenching and sustaining— until the next snack, that is!

Names like *es kopyor*, *es campur*, *es tape* and *es Bandung* may give little indication of their contents to the uninitiated. About the only constant factor is that they contain some shaved or crushed ice (*es*).

Stalls and mobile carts sell a wide selection of special Indonesian drinks mixed with ice (es) as well as bottled carbonated drinks.

Some ice drinks may be made largely from tropical fruits such as soursop (*sirsak*), avocado, banana and papaya, mashed with a spoon or blended with milk, ice and sweetening. Incidentally, in Indonesia, avocado (*apokat*) is regarded as a fruit and eaten with sugar, or even made into ice cream.

Others drinks might include fermented rice or cassava (*tape*), slivers of young coconut, chunks or strips of colorful gelatin, dried red beans, sweet corn kernels, vivid green "noodles" of transparent mung pea flour and even chunks of bread. These are combined with either rose-flavored syrup, palm sugar syrup or sweetened condensed milk— there are countless roads to sweetness.

Less complex coolers are the brightly colored and often excessively sweet cordials known by their Dutch name, *stroop*. One of the nicest is made from passion fruit (*markisa*), grown in hilly areas in Bali, Java, Sumatra and Sulawesi. *Jeruk* is is term for any citrus fruit and *es jeruk* is normally the juice of local green-skinned oranges.

Plantations of coffee and tea were important contributors to the colonial coffers during the 19th century and remain valuable crops today. Tea in Indonesia means one of two things: *air teh* (literally tea water), usually served with meals, is nothing more than boiling water faintly flavored with tea, while tea consumed on its own or with a light snack in a *warung* or *rumah makan* will invariably be sweet and milky.

Coffee is more popular than tea in many areas of Indonesia. Coffee beans are frequently dark roasted and ground with a little corn. Rather than being brewed, filtered, percolated or otherwise mechanically manipulated, finely ground coffee is put straight into the serving glass and mixed with boiling water. The trick of drinking the coffee (known as *kopi tobruk*) without getting a mouthful of grounds is to stir it a little so that the grounds settle. Indonesians love sugar and coffee is automatically served sweet unless one asks for it *pahit* (literally "bitter").

Stronger drinks can almost always be found, except in conservative Islamic areas (Muslims are forbidden to drink alcohol). Two popular local brands of beer, Bintang and Anker, are made to Dutch specifications and are similar to any European lager beer. Most Westerners looking for a beverage to accompany Indonesian food will find that beer is the perfect drink.

In many non-Muslim areas, a local brew is made from either rice or the sap of the coconut or *lontar* palm. Bali is noted for its *brem*, a sweetish drink that

A range of popular drinks includes iced young coconut, iced orange juice, rose-flavored es bandung *and* green cendol.

is basically a type of rice beer. Sticky rice is favored for rice wine; in parts of Kalimantan, it is still made in valuable heirloom jars brought by the Chinese as trade goods centuries ago.

Palm wine is made by tapping the sap that flows from the inflorescence of the coconut or *lontar* palm. The toddy is enjoyed fresh the day it is gathered, or left to mature for a few days; leftovers are distilled to made a fierce *arak* or brandy.

Part Two: The Indonesian Kitchen

A combination of simplicity and practicality

One of the many surprising aspects of Indonesia is the way such delicious food, often a complex blending of herbs, spices and seasonings come out of the simplest of kitchens. The gleaming modern designer kitchen with tiled surfaces, electrical appliances and hot and cold running water is unknown to the majority of Indonesians. Kitchens are functional rather than aesthetic, with meals cooked over a wood fire or a *kompor*, a kerosene burner. In urban areas, gas burners fueled by LPG are increasingly used.

Preparing Indonesian food in your own kitchen does not require a complex array of ingredients, but there are certain utensils that will make the task a lot easier. First and foremost you need something to grind or crush the seasonings (*bumbu*) that form the basis of countless Indonesian dishes and are also used as condiments or *sambals*.

In Indonesia, a saucer-shaped granite **grinding stone** together with a **granite pestle** are used for this task. Unlike neighboring Malaysia and Thailand, where ingredients are pounded with a pestle inside a deep mortar, the Indonesian cook rubs or grinds ingredients with a backwards and forwards motion across the granite.

Although a mortar and pestle is very useful for dealing with small amounts of ingredients, most modern cooks will find a **food processor**, **blender** or even **coffee grinder** the easiest way to prepare the basic spice paste or *bumbu*. (See page 32.)

Also important is a **chopping board** and **cleaver**. This duo performs a myriad of tasks: chopping up chicken into the required size; cutting vegetables; finely mincing meat or fish in the absence of a food processor; using the flat side of the cleaver to bruise lemongrass, cardamom pods or garlic (to remove the garlic skin), and so on. In Asia, a thick cross section of a hard tree is used; this type of board is durable and functional. Choose the biggest board available, with a cleaver with a blade 3–4 inches deep.

A **wok**, basically a conical frying pan, is infinitely preferable to a frying pan for many dishes. Known as a *kuali* (or, in Java, *wajan*), this versatile utensil is practical for deep frying (it uses less oil) and also allows just the right amount of evaporation for many dishes which begin with a large amount of liquid and finish with a thick sauce. When choosing a

Opposite:
Terra-cotta cooking pans piled in the center of this Javanese man's bicycle on their way to market.
Bottom right:
Traditional pottery is still used in Indonesian kitchens.

Spoons made of wood or coconut shell are put to countless uses in an Indonesian kitchen.

wok, avoid aluminum or Teflon-coated types.

A heavy cast-iron wok that won't tip over easily is preferable, or best of all, the Rolls Royce of woks, which is made of a nonstick alloy that will not scratch when metal scoops are used.

To partner your wok, a **frying shovel** or **metal spatula**, as well as a **perforated ladle** for lifting out deep-fried food, are useful. Indonesian cooks also use an assortment of wooden or coconut husk spoons for stirring.

It is important not to use aluminum or cast-iron saucepans for cooking Indonesian food. Many recipes contain acidic ingredients, such as tamarind juice or lime, or white coconut milk, and using aluminum or cast iron will result in a discolored sauce or cause a chemical reaction. Choose either stainless steel, teflon-coated, glass or enameled **saucepans**.

Bundles of banana-leaf-wrapped food are often steamed, usually put inside the conical basket used to steam rice. The most practical approach in a Western kitchen is to buy a two-tiered Chinese woven **bamboo steamer** with a cover. This steamer sits inside a wok just above the level of boiling water. The bamboo is ideal, as it absorbs the moisture rather than letting it fall back into the food. Dry the steamer and lid thoroughly before storing.

An alternative to the bamboo steamer is a **perforated metal disc** that sits inside a wok above the level of boiling water; however, this will not hold as much food as a two-tiered steamer, and you will need to find a convex lid that fits over your wok.

One item widely used in Indonesian cooking is seldom easily available outside the tropics. This is the multi-purpose **banana leaf**, used for wrapping food for grilling, steaming, or placing directly onto hot coals.

Just to give some idea of the versatility of the banana leaf, one Indonesian cooking manual illustrates 24 different ways of wrapping food in banana leaf, depending on the contents and the particular style of preparation!

If you are able to obtain banana leaf, wipe it clean and cut to the required size. Hold it directly over a gas flame or plunge in boiling water until it softens before wrapping the food. Sadly, substitutes for banana leaf just don't reproduce the subtle flavor and texture of the real thing.

Aluminum foil is generally recommended, but for a texture that is closer to that obtained by using the banana leaf, wrap food in parchment paper first, then in the foil.

DOUBLE-WRAPPED BANANA LEAF PACKET

Step 1: *place ingredients in center of clean leaf and pleat in side as shown*

Step 2: *repeat on other side*

Step 3: *fold one end of pleat to the front and the other to the back*

Step 4: *repeat on other side to firmly enclose contents*

Step 5: *put bundle in center of strip of leaf and fold up to hold the pleats together*

Step 6: *secure with a toothpick*

SIMPLE BANANA LEAF ROLL (PEPES)

Step 1: *place ingredients along the piece of clean leaf as shown*

Step 2: *roll over firmly*

Step 3: *secure both ends of the roll with toothpicks*

Cooking Methods

Preparing the all-important
spice paste and coconut milk

Indonesian food is prepared in a variety of ways: pan-fried or deep fried, grilled over hot coals, simmered, steamed and even—in remote areas of Irian Jaya—baked in an earth oven as in Polynesia.

It is essential to master the art of preparing the **basic spice paste** or *bumbu* used to season so many dishes. Indonesian cooks use a grinding stone; ingredients are peeled if necessary and, where relevant, sliced or chopped into small pieces before being ground. If you are using a blender or food processor, the order of processing the spices is much the same as for a grinding stone, but you will probably need to add some liquid to keep the blades of the machine turning during the blending process. If the spice paste is to be fried, add just a little of the specified amount of oil to the food processor. If the spice paste is to be simmered in either coconut milk, stock or water, add a little of this instead.

The order to be followed when grinding or processing spice paste ingredients is hard items first: dried spices, nuts and tough fibrous rhizomes or leaves, such as galangal and lemongrass. When these are fine, add softer rhizomes, such as turmeric, ginger and fresh or soaked dried chilies. Process until fine, then add ingredients that are full of moisture, such as shallots and garlic. Finally, add

A granite mortar and pestle is used to grind the basic spice paste or bumbu, *but a food processor does the job far more quickly and effortlessly.*

shrimp paste and tamarind juice and process just to mix well.

The spice paste is then either fried in oil or simmered in liquid. If it is to be fried, put it in oil over low to moderate heat and fry, stirring from time to time, until it starts to smell fragrant. This takes from 3–5 minutes. Often, pieces of meat or poultry are added to the spice paste and stir fried until they are well coated and the color has changed. Coconut milk is frequently added at this stage and the liquid brought to a boil before the heat is lowered and the food simmered until done.

When cooking with **coconut milk**, it is important to prevent it from curdling or breaking apart. First, stir the milk frequently, lifting it up with a large spoon or ladle and pouring it back into the saucepan or wok, while it is coming to a boil. Once the coconut milk is simmering, be sure never to cover the pan. Thick coconut milk is sometimes added at the final stages to thicken and enrich the flavor of the dish. Stir constantly while heating but do not allow to boil.

Rice

*A meal is not a meal without rice,
the staple which also has profound ritual significance*

Rice, the physical mainstay of millions of Indonesians, is far more than just a staple food. The plant is perceived to have a soul or spirit and is therefore subject to many ritual observances during growth and harvesting.

Although there are dozens of varieties of rice in Indonesia, the most common fall into two basic categories: **long-grain polished white rice** and **glutinous rice**. The former is eaten as a staple, while glutinous rice is used to make desserts, cakes and snacks. Glutinous or sticky rice (*ketan* or *pulot*) is either white or purplish-black (*pulot hitam*), with a wonderfully nutty flavor.

Cooking rice is a subject that often arouses controversy, and if you already have a favorite method, stick with it. Whatever method is used, it is essential to first wash the rice thoroughly to remove any impurities and starch clinging to the grains; failure to do this may result in soggy rice. Put the rice into a saucepan, half fill with water, rub the grains for a few seconds, then tip off the water. Repeat this step as many times as necessary until the water runs clear. Drain.

The absorbency of rice depends on the variety of rice and its age, with older rice absorbing more liquid. Cooking times depend on the type and weight of your saucepan, and the heat of your cooker. The following absorption method is used by millions throughout Asia.

PLAIN RICE (*NASI PUTIH*)

Measure a minimum of $1/2$ cup of uncooked rice per person and wash thoroughly. Put into a heavy-bottomed pan with enough water to cover the rice and come up to the level of the first joint on your forefinger (about $3/4$ inch). Cover the pan and bring to a boil over high heat. Set the lid slightly to one side, lower heat slightly and simmer until all the water is absorbed and dimples or "craters" appear in the top of the rice. Reduce heat to the absolute minimum, cover the pan and leave the rice to cook for at least another 10 minutes. Remove the lid, fluff up the rice with a fork (do **not** stir before this), wipe any condensation off the lid and recover the pan. Set aside until required. The rice should keep warm for at least another 15–20 minutes.

A traditional rice steamer or kukusan.

Indonesian Ingredients

*The cook as artist: an essential
palette of herbs, spices and seasonings*

Basil

Carambola

Candlenuts

Many Indonesian ingredients are now widely available in Asian supply shops, mail-order speciality shops (see page 118), and even supermarkets abroad. Essential ingredients are described for easy identification, and a range of substitutes suggested.

ANCHOVIES, DRIED (*ikan teri*): Small salted dried anchovies are used to season some dishes. Available in most Chinese stores. Unless they are very tiny, anchovies are usually less than 1 inch long. Discard the heads and any black intestinal tract before frying.

BASIL (*daun selasih, daun kemangi*): Two varieties of this fragrant herb are found in Indonesia. They are generally added to dishes at the last minute for maximum flavor. *Daun kemangi* has a lemony scent, while *daun selasih* (identical to Thai *horapa*) is more similar to sweet European basil, which can be used as a substitute.

BEAN CURD (*tahu*): Bean curd, introduced by the Chinese, is now widely used in vegetable dishes and salads, providing inexpensive protein. Bean curd is sold in cakes about 3 inches square. This bean curd is sometimes compressed to expel much of the moisture, forming **hard bean curd cakes**. Do not confuse regular bean curd with soft or "silken" bean curd sold in many stores abroad; this is commonly used for Chinese soups and in Japanese cuisine.

CANDLENUT (*buah kemiri*): A round, cream-colored nut related to the macadamia, this has an oily consistency used to add texture and a faint flavor to many dishes. Store in the refrigerator as candlenuts turn rancid quickly. Substitute with macadamia nuts or raw cashews.

CARAMBOLA, SOUR (*belimbing wuluh*): This pale green acidic fruit about 2–3 inches long grows in clusters on a tree. A relative of the large, five-edged sweet starfruit, carambola is used whole or sliced to give a sour tang to some soups, fish dishes and *sambals*. Sour grapefruit or tamarind juice can be used as a substitute.

CARDAMOM (*kepulaga*): About 8–12 intensely fragrant black seeds are enclosed in a straw-colored, fibrous pod. Try to buy the whole pod rather than cardamom seeds or powder for maximum flavor, and bruise lightly with the back of a cleaver to break the pod before adding to food.

CELERY (*selderi*): The celery used in Indonesia is different from the normal Western variety, with slender stems and particularly pungent leaves. It is often referred to as "Chinese celery" abroad and is used as a herb rather than a vegetable.

CHILIES (*cabai*, also called *cabe* or *lombok*): Several types of chili pepper are used, with the amount of heat increasing as the size diminishes. **Green chilies** are the unripe fruit, and have a flavor different from ripe **red chilies**. Fresh, finger-length red chilies are the most commonly used; these are also dried and used in some dishes, especially in Sumatra. **Dried chilies** should be torn into pieces and soaked in hot water to soften before grinding or blending. Hottest of all chilies are the tiny fiery **bird's-eye chilies** (*cabai rawit*).

To reduce the heat of a dish while retaining the flavor, remove some or all of the seeds. Be careful to wash your hands thoroughly after handling chilies as the oil can burn your eyes and skin. You may even like to wear rubber gloves.

CHIVES, COARSE (*kucai*): Sometimes called "garlic chives," the flat 12-inch long leaves are used as a seasoning. Although the flavor is more delicate, spring onions (scallions) can be used as a substitute.

CINNAMON (*kayu manis*): The thick, dark brown bark of a type of cassia is used in Indonesia, not true cinnamon. The latter is more subtle in flavor and considerably more expensive. Always use whole bark, not ground cinnamon.

CLOVES (*cengkeh*): This small, brown, nail-shaped spice was once found only in the islands of Maluku. Cloves are used in cooking less frequently than one might expect, but add their characteristic fragrance to the clove-scented cigarettes or *kretek* popular throughout Indonesia.

COCONUT (*kelapa*): Coconuts are widely used in Indonesia, not just in cooking but also for palm sugar, alcohol, housing, utensils and charcoal. The grated flesh of the coconut is frequently added to food; it is also squeezed with water to make coconut milk.

To make **fresh coconut milk**, put the flesh of 1 freshly grated ripe coconut into a bowl and add ½ cup of lukewarm water. Squeeze and knead the coconut thoroughly for 1 minute, then squeeze handful by handful, straining into a bowl to obtain thick coconut milk. Repeat the process with another 2½ cups of water to obtain thin coconut milk. Combine thin and thick milk for the coconut milk called for in recipes in this book, unless thick coconut milk is specified.

Coconut milk can be frozen; thaw and stir thoroughly before use. The best substitute for fresh coconut milk to be used with vegetables,

Chinese Celery

Chilies

Coconut

Coarse Chives

Cinnamon

Galangal

Kencur

Lemongrass

seafood, meat and for sauces is **instant coconut powder**, sometimes sold under the name "santan." Combine this with warm water as directed on the packet. For the richer, creamier flavor required for desserts and cakes, use **canned (unsweetened) coconut cream**.

CORIANDER (*ketumbar*): Small straw-colored seeds with a faintly orange flavor, coriander is one of the most commonly used spices in Indonesia. It is often used in conjunction with white pepper and cumin.

CUMIN (*jinten*): Together with coriander and pepper, this small beige elongated seed is one of the most commonly used spices in Indonesia. Take care not to confuse it with fennel.

FENNEL (*jinten manis*): This seed is similar to cumin, although slightly fatter, whiter, and with a distinctive fragrance reminiscent of aniseed.

GALANGAL (*laos*): A member of the ginger family with a very tough but elusively scented rhizome, which must be peeled before use. The best substitute is water-packed slices of galangal sold in jars, generally exported from Thailand. Otherwise, use slices of dried *laos* (soaked in boiling water for 30 minutes) or, as a last resort, powdered *laos* (1 teaspoon = 1 inch).

GARLIC (*bawang putih*): Recipes in this book were prepared with Indonesian garlic, the cloves of which are usually smaller and less pungent than the garlic found in many Western countries. Adjust the amount to suit your taste.

GINGER (*jahe*): This pale creamy yellow root is widely used, not just to season food but for its medicinal properties (it helps digestion, expels intestinal gas, improves the appetite and is believed to be good for colds). Always scrape the skin off fresh ginger before using, and do not substitute powdered ginger as the taste is quite different. Fresh ginger keeps in a cool place for several weeks.

JICAMA (*bengkuang*): Native to tropical America, the jicama, or yam bean as it is sometimes known, is actually a tuber with a beige skin and crisp white interior. It is used in salads and some cooked vegetable dishes; water chestnuts make an acceptable substitute.

KENARI: A soft, somewhat oily nut found in Maluku; almond is the closest substitute.

KENCUR: Sometimes incorrectly known as lesser galangal, the botanical name of this ginger-like root is *Kaemferia galanga*. The correct English name, rarely encountered, is zedoary. *Kencur* has a unique, camphor-like flavor and should be used sparingly. Wash it and, if you're fussy (most Indonesians aren't), scrape off the skin before using. Dried sliced *kencur* (sometimes spelled *kentjoer*) or *kencur* powder can be used as a substitute. Soak dried slices in boiling water for 30 minutes; use $1/2$–1 teaspoon of powder for 1 inch of fresh root.

KRUPUK: Dried crackers made from shrimp, fish, vegetables or nuts mixed with various types of flour are enormously popular as a garnish or snack. They must be thoroughly dry before deep frying in very hot oil for a few seconds, so that they puff up and become crisp.

LEMONGRASS (*serai, sereh*): This intensely fragrant herb is used to impart a lemony flavor to many dishes and can also be used as a skewer for satays. Cut off the roots and use only the tender bottom portion (6–8 inches). Discard the hard outer leaves. If a whole stem is added to a sauce during cooking, it should be bruised a couple of times with the edge of a cleaver or a pestle to release the fragrance, then tied in a knot to hold it together.

LIME: Several types of lime are used in Indonesia. The most fragrant is the leprous or **kaffir lime** (*jeruk purut*). It has virtually no juice, but the double leaf is often used whole or very finely shredded, while the grated skin is occasionally used in cooking. Round **yellow-skinned limes** slightly larger than a golf ball (*jeruk nipis*) and small, **dark green limes** (*jeruk limau*) are used for their juice. If limes are not available, use lemons.

NOODLES (*mi, mie*): Introduced by the Chinese and a firm favorite everywhere. The most common varieties are fresh spaghetti-like yellow egg noodles (*bami*) and **dried rice vermicelli** (*mihun*). Transparent noodles made from mung pea flour (*sohun*), called **cellophane noodles** in the West, are used in some soup and vegetable dishes for texture rather than flavor.

NUTMEG (*pala*): Always grate whole nutmeg just before using as the powdered spice quickly loses its fragrance. Whole nutmegs keep almost indefinitely.

PALM SUGAR (*gula merah, gula Jawa*): Juice extracted from coconut or *aren* palm flowers is boiled and packed into molds to make sugar with a faint caramel taste. If palm sugar is not available, substitute soft brown sugar or a mixture of brown sugar and maple syrup.

To make **palm sugar syrup**, combine equal amounts of chopped palm sugar and water, adding a pandan leaf if available. Bring to a boil, simmer for 10 minutes, strain and store in refrigerator.

PANDAN LEAF (*daun pandan*): The fragrant leaf of a type of pandanus sometimes known as fragrant screwpine is tied in a knot and used to flavor some curries, desserts and cakes. Bottled pandan essence can be substituted.

PEANUTS (*kacang tanah*): These are ground (either raw or cooked) and used to make sauces; deep-fried peanuts are a very common garnish or condiment. Do not salt fried peanuts before storing to avoid their becoming soggy.

Kaffir Lime

Limes

Palm Sugar

Pandan Leaf

Salam Leaf

Dried Shrimp Paste

Shallots

Spring Onion

PEPPER (*merica, lada*): Whole black or white peppercorns are generally crushed just before use; ground white pepper is also used on certain occasions.

PRAWNS, DRIED (*ebi*): Used to season some dishes, these should be soaked in warm water for 5 minutes before use and any shells discarded. Choose dried prawns that are bright pink in color, avoiding any that look grey or moldy.

SALAM LEAF (*daun salam*): A subtly flavored leaf of a member of the cassia family. The flavor bears no resemblance whatsoever to that of bay leaves, which are sometimes suggested as a substitute. If you cannot obtain dried *salam* leaf, omit altogether.

SALTED SOY BEANS (*tauco*): Salty and with a distinctive tang, this Chinese ingredient is used to season some dishes and to make a savory side dish or *sambal*. Available in jars, sometimes labeled "Yellow Bean Sauce."

SHALLOTS (*bawang merah*): Widely used throughout Indonesia, shallots are sliced and eaten raw in *sambals*, pounded to make spice pastes, sliced and added during cooking or sliced and deep fried to make Indonesia's most popular garnish. Packets of deep-fried shallots are generally available in Asian supply stores. If they lose their crispness, scatter in a large baking dish and put in a very low oven for a few moments to dry them thoroughly. Cool thoroughly before storing.

Indonesian shallots are smaller and milder than those found in many Western countries, so you may need to reduce the amount called for in these recipes.

SHRIMP PASTE, BLACK (*petis*): A very thick syrupy paste, usually sold in jars or plastic tubs, with a strong shrimp flavor, *petis* is used to season some sauces; perhaps best known as an ingredient in Rojak, a fruit and vegetable salad drenched with a hot, sour, faintly fishy sauce.

SHRIMP PASTE, DRIED (*trasi*): This very pungent seasoning often smells offensive to the uninitiated. It is always cooked before eating, which kills the smell and greatly improves the flavor. The best way to prepare shrimp paste is to spread the required amount on a piece of foil and to toast it under a grill or dry fry in a pan for about 2 minutes on each side. If you prefer to avoid the pungent smell during cooking, wrap in the edges of the foil before cooking. If the shrimp paste is to be fried with other spice paste ingredients, it does not need precooking.

Widely known overseas by its Indonesian name, *trasi*, or the Malay term, *belacan*, shrimp paste ranges in color from purplish pink to beige to brownish black and is generally sold in a cake.

SOY SAUCE: Two types of soy sauce are used in Indonesia: **thick sweet soy sauce** (*kecap manis*), which is most frequently used as a condiment, usually with added sliced chilies, and the thinner, saltier **light soy sauce** (*kecap asin*). If you cannot obtain *kecap manis*, use thick black Chinese soy sauce and add brown sugar to sweeten it.

SPRING ONION (*daun bawang*): Sometimes known as scallion, this popular herb is often used as a garnish and to add flavor to many dishes.

STAR ANISE (*bunga lawang*): An 8-pointed star-shaped spice, dark brown in color, with each point containing a shiny brown round seed, this has a strong aniseed or licorice flavor.

TAMARIND (*asam Jawa*): The pod of the tamarind tree contains seeds covered by a fleshy pulp, which adds fruity sourness to many dishes. Packets of dried tamarind pulp usually contain the seeds and fibers. To make **tamarind juice**, measure 1 part of pulp and soak it in 3 parts of hot water for 5 minutes before squeezing it to extract the juice, discarding the seeds, fiber and any skin.

TAPIOCA (*ubi kayu*): The root of this plant, also known as cassava, and the tender green leaves are both used as a vegetable. The root is also grated and mixed with coconut and sugar to make a number of cakes. Fermented tapioca root is added to some dessert dishes, while the dried root is made into small balls and used in the same way as pearl sago. Substitute spinach for tapioca leaves.

TEMPEH: This Javanese creation, cakes of compressed, lightly fermented soy beans, is increasingly known to health enthusiasts internationally. It is rich in protein and has a delicious nutty flavor. Often available in health food stores. No substitute.

TURMERIC (*kunyit*): A vivid yellow rhizome of the ginger family, this has a very emphatic flavor. Scrape the skin before using. If fresh turmeric is not available, substitute 1 teaspoon of powdered turmeric for 1 inch of the fresh root. The leaf of the turmeric plant is sometimes used as a herb, particularly in Sumatra. There is no substitute.

WATER SPINACH (*kangkung*): Sometimes known as Morning Glory or Swamp Cabbage, this aquatic plant is full of nutrition and has an excellent flavor. Often steamed and used in many salads with a spicy sauce. The tender leaves and tips of the plant are used, and the tough hollow stems discarded. Available in most Chinese markets, often under the Cantonese name, *ong choy*.

Star Anise

Turmeric

Water Spinach

Jicama

Part Three: The Recipes

Recipes for accompaniments and sambals
precede those for the main dishes, which begin on page 46

In Indonesia, as in most of Asia, food is seldom served in individual portions. Rice and other dishes are placed on the table for people to help themselves. It is thus difficult to estimate the exact number of portions each recipe will provide. As a general rule, recipes in this book will serve 4–6 people as part of a meal with rice and three other dishes.

ACCOMPANIMENTS

Serundeng • *Spiced Coconut with Peanuts*

2 shallots, peeled and sliced
2 cloves garlic, peeled and sliced
2 teaspoons chopped palm sugar
1 teaspoon dried shrimp paste (*trasi*), toasted
1 tablespoon tamarind juice
4 cups freshly grated or unsweetened dried
   coconut
2/3 cup fried peanuts, skinned

Grind or blend the shallots, garlic, palm sugar, shrimp paste and tamarind juice. Mix well with coconut and put into a wok. Dry fry over low heat, stirring constantly, until golden and crisp. Add fried peanuts and allow to cool. Keeps for weeks stored in an airtight container. Sprinkle with a little salt and mix only just before serving to ensure the Serundeng remains crisp.

Ingredients

When a recipe lists a hard-to-find or unusual ingredient, see pages 34 to 39 for possible substitutes. If a substitute is not listed, look for the ingredient in your local Asian food market, or check the mail-order listings on page 118 for possible sources.

Time Estimates

Time estimates are for preparation only (excluding cooking) and are based on the assumption that a food processor or blender will be used.

🕐 *quick and very easy to prepare*

🕐🕐 *relatively easy; less than 15 minutes to prepare*

🕐🕐🕐 *takes more than 15 minutes to prepare*

Opposite:
A selection of Acar or pickles. Clockwise from top: Acar Bawang, Acar Cabe, Acar Segar & Acar Mentimun.

Dabu Dabu Kenari •
Pickled Cucumber and Bean Sprouts

1 medium-sized cucumber (about 8 ounces),
   peeled and sliced
1 cup bean sprouts, blanched
4 shallots, finely sliced
3 red chilies, sliced
5 bird's-eye chilies, sliced
4 sprigs basil
$\frac{1}{3}$ cup *kenari* nuts or raw almonds, peeled and
   coarsely ground
3 tablespoons lime or lemon juice
$\frac{1}{2}$ teaspoon white sugar
$\frac{1}{2}$ teaspoon dried shrimp paste (*trasi*), toasted
$\frac{1}{2}$ teaspoon salt

Arrange cucumber and bean sprouts on a plate and
sprinkle with shallots, chilies and basil. Combine
nuts, lime juice, sugar, shrimp paste and salt,
adding a little warm water to make a thick sauce.
Pour sauce over vegetables and serve.

*Sambal Mangga
served in* daun
mangkokan, *a
decorative leaf
used as a herb
in Sumatra.*

Acar Bawang • *Pickled Shallots*

2 tablespoons white vinegar
1 teaspoon salt
$1\frac{1}{2}$ tablespoons white sugar
3 tablespoons warm water
24 shallots, peeled and sliced

Mix all ingredients except shallots, stirring until
sugar dissolves. Combine with shallots and sliced
chili, if desired. Leave 2–3 hours before serving.

Acar Cabe • *Pickled Chilies*

$1\frac{1}{2}$ tablespoons white sugar
2 tablespoons white vinegar
1 teaspoon salt
$2\frac{1}{2}$ tablespoons warm water
30 red or green bird's-eye chilies, sliced

Mix sugar, vinegar, salt and water until sugar dissolves. Combine with chilies and leave for 2–3 hours
before use. Keeps refrigerated up to 1 week.

Acar Mentimun • *Cucumber Pickles*

1 tablespoon white vinegar
$2\frac{1}{2}$ tablespoons white sugar
1 teaspoon salt
$2\frac{1}{2}$ tablespoons hot water
1 medium-sized cucumber, peeled, seeded, cut
   lengthwise, then sliced

Mix vinegar, sugar, salt and water until sugar dissolves, then combine with cucumber and allow to
rest 1 hour before serving.

Acar Segar • *Vegetable Pickles*

1 small cucumber, peeled, seeded and cut in
   matchsticks
1 carrot, peeled and cut in matchsticks

12 shallots, peeled and quartered
$1^1/_2$ cups water
3 tablespoons vinegar
1 tablespoon sugar
1 teaspoon salt

Combine vegetables. Mix water, vinegar, sugar and salt and combine with vegetables. Refrigerate several hours before use.

SAMBALS

Sambal Bajak • *Fragrant Chili Sambal*

7 red chilies, seeded and sliced
$^1/_4$ teaspoon freshly grated nutmeg
1 teaspoon dried shrimp paste (*trasi*), toasted
6 shallots, peeled and sliced
3 cloves garlic, peeled and sliced
1 teaspoon salt
$1^1/_2$ teaspoons chopped palm sugar
2 tablespoons oil
2 *salam* leaves
2 stalks lemongrass, bruised
$^1/_2$ inch galangal (*laos*), peeled and sliced
4 tablespoons tamarind juice

Combine first 7 ingredients and grind or blend finely. Heat oil and sauté ground ingredients together with *salam* leaves, lemongrass and galangal, stirring until the mixture changes color. Add tamarind juice and simmer for another minute, then leave to cool. Remove *salam* leaves, lemongrass and galangal before serving. Keeps up to 1 week.

Sambal Bawang • *Shallot Sambal*

$1^1/_2$ cups oil
25 shallots, peeled and sliced

10 red chilies, seeded and sliced
7 cloves garlic, peeled and sliced
1 teaspoon salt
1 tablespoon dried shrimp paste (*trasi*), toasted
1 tablespoon lime or lemon juice

Heat oil and sauté all ingredients, except for lime juice, over high heat for 2 minutes. Cool, then add lime juice. Keeps up to 1 week.

Sambal Goreng Jipang • *Chayote Sambal*

13 red chilies, seeded and sliced
12 shallots, peeled and sliced
7 cloves garlic, peeled and sliced
6 candlenuts
1 inch galangal (*laos*), peeled and chopped
2 tablespoons oil
$3^1/_2$ ounces dried prawns, soaked
1 teaspoon brown sugar
3 cups coconut milk
3 *salam* leaves
$^1/_2$ teaspoon salt
1 pound chayote or zucchini, peeled and sliced

Grind or blend chilies, shallots, garlic, candlenuts and galangal to a coarse paste. Heat oil in wok and sauté the spice paste for 1 minute. Add dried prawns and sugar and continue sautéing until the mixture is fragrant. Put in the coconut milk together with *salam* leaves and salt and bring almost to a boil. Add the vegetable and simmer until just tender, stirring from time to time.

Sambal Kecap, as simple as it is ubiquitous.

Sambal Kecap • *Sweet Soy Sauce Sambal*

2 red chilies, seeded and sliced
4 shallots, peeled and sliced
2 tablespoons sweet soy sauce

Mix all ingredients well and serve.

Sambal Lada Hijau • *Green Chili and Dried Anchovy Sambal*

$\frac{1}{2}$ cup dried anchovies (*ikan teri*)
1 cup oil
4 shallots, peeled and sliced
6 green bird's-eye chilies, sliced
2 medium-sized tomatoes, seeded and diced

Remove heads and black intestinal tract from dried anchovies if they have not already been cleaned. Heat all but 1 tablespoon of the oil and fry the anchovies until crisp and golden brown. Drain and set aside. Clean pan, then add remaining oil and fry shallots, chilies and tomatoes until soft. Combine with fried anchovies and serve with steamed rice.

Sambal Luat • *Jicama Sambal*

1 jicama (*bengkuang*) (about 4 ounces), or
 10–12 water chestnuts, peeled and diced
10–15 red chilies, sliced
$\frac{1}{2}$ teaspoon dried shrimp paste (*trasi*), toasted
2 cloves garlic
$\frac{1}{2}$ teaspoon salt
1$\frac{1}{2}$ tablespoons lime or lemon juice
2 sprigs basil

Put jicama in a bowl. Grind or blend the chilies, shrimp paste, garlic, salt and lime juice. Mix with jicama and garnish with basil.

Sambal Manbo • *Sour Sambal*

1 tablespoon oil
5 shallots, peeled and sliced
2 cloves garlic, peeled and sliced
6 bird's-eye chilies, chopped
6 small sour carambola (*belimbing wuluh*) or
 2 tablespoons tamarind juice
1$\frac{1}{2}$ cups fried peanuts, coarsely ground
1 teaspoon dried shrimp paste (*trasi*), toasted
4 tablespoons sweet soy sauce
1 teaspoon salt
1 green tomato, sliced
2 cucumbers, peeled and sliced

Heat oil and sauté shallots and garlic until soft, then add chilies, carambola, peanuts, shrimp paste and soy sauce. Cook over low heat until the carambola is soft. If using tamarind juice, simmer 1 minute only. Season with salt and serve with tomato and cucumbers. Good with grilled fish.

Sambal Mangga • *Mango Sambal*

1 pound unripe green mangoes, peeled and
 finely chopped
1 tablespoon salt
10 shallots, peeled and chopped
6 red chilies, sliced
4 green chilies, sliced
1 teaspoon dried shrimp paste (*trasi*), toasted
1 sprig basil, chopped
$\frac{1}{4}$ cup coconut or other oil

Sprinkle mangoes with salt and set aside for 10–15 minutes. Squeeze out sour juices. Grind shallots, chilies and shrimp paste. Mix with basil and oil, then combine with mangoes.

Sambal Soto • *Soup Sambal*

5 candlenuts, deep-fried whole until golden
10 shallots, peeled and sliced
20 bird's-eye chilies, sliced
2–3 cloves garlic
$\frac{1}{4}$ teaspoon salt
1 teaspoon white sugar
$\frac{3}{4}$ cup lime or lemon juice

Grind or blend first 4 ingredients. Add salt, sugar and lime juice. Mix well and serve with noodle soups.

Sambal Tauco • *Salted Soy Bean Sambal*

$\frac{1}{2}$ cup salted soy beans (*tauco*)
$\frac{1}{2}$ cup coconut milk
Salt to taste

Spice Paste:

6 shallots, peeled and sliced
3 cloves garlic, peeled and sliced
5 green chilies, sliced
2 tablespoons oil
1 stalk lemongrass, bruised
2 *salam* leaves
1 tablespoon tamarind juice
$\frac{1}{2}$ teaspoon chopped palm sugar

Grind or blend shallots, garlic and chilies. Heat oil and fry ground paste together with all other **spice paste** ingredients until fragrant. Add salted soy beans and sauté for another minute, then add coconut milk and simmer, stirring, until thickened. Add salt to taste and cool before serving.

Sambal Trasi • *Sambal with Shrimp Paste*

12 red chilies, seeded and sliced
2 tablespoons dried shrimp paste (*trasi*), toasted
1 medium-sized tomato, seeded and finely chopped
$1\frac{1}{2}$ tablespoons chopped palm sugar
1 tablespoon lime or lemon juice

Combine all ingredients and grind or blend well. For a more fiery *sambal*, use bird's-eye chilies.

Below: *A platter of Sambals. Clockwise from the top: Sambal Bawang, Sambal Lada Hijau, Sambal Goreng Jipang, Sambal Luat, Sambal Soto, Sambal Trasi, Sambal Manbo and Sambal Bajak, with Dabu Dabu Kenari in the center.*

ASAM UDANG & SAMBAL TAPPA

Marinated Sour Shrimp & Sour Mango and Tuna Sambal

ASAM UDANG

Belimbing wuluh, small sour carambola fruits, grow abundantly in many kitchen gardens throughout Indonesia, as well as in other areas of Southeast Asia. They add a delicious tang to this North Sumatran salad, although sour grapefruit or sour oranges can be used as a substitute. ✆

Opposite:
*Asam Udang
(top left) and
Sambal Tappa
(bottom right).*

2 pounds large shrimp (with shell)
6 shallots, peeled and finely chopped
3 red chilies, seeded and finely sliced
4 sour carambola (*belimbing wuluh*), sliced, or
   1 sour grapefruit, peeled and chopped

Put shrimp in a pan with 8 cups of water and bring to a boil. Simmer for 4 minutes, drain and plunge shrimp in ice water for 30 seconds. Drain, then peel shrimp.

Grind or blend shallots, chilies and carambola or grapefruit to a fine paste. Taste and add a little lime or lemon juice if not sour enough. Combine with shrimp and serve.

SAMBAL TAPPA

This recipe comes from Ambon, in Maluku, where tuna is abundant. Although the flavor is not as good, drained canned tuna can be used as a substitute, if fresh tuna is not available. ✆

5 sour green mangoes, peeled and coarsely
   shredded
2 teaspoons salt
$1\frac{1}{4}$ pounds fresh tuna, grilled and flaked
3 shallots, peeled and sliced
1 teaspoon white peppercorns, ground
$\frac{1}{4}$ cup thick coconut milk

Mix mangoes with salt and set aside for 10 minutes. Squeeze to remove sour liquid. Mix with the tuna, shallots, pepper and coconut milk and serve.

KAREDOK & LOTEK

Raw Vegetables & Cooked Vegetables in Peanut Sauce

KAREDOK

The Sundanese of West Java are renowned for their love of vegetables, both raw and cooked, and often eat them as between-meal snacks. They can, of course, be served with rice as part of a main meal. ⏱ ⏱

1/4 medium-sized round green cabbage, shredded
1 small cucumber, peeled, halved lengthwise and sliced
2 cups bean sprouts, cleaned
4 tiny round eggplants, or 1 small long eggplant, finely sliced
1 cup diced young long beans
4 sprigs basil
Fried shallots and prawn wafers (*krupuk*) to garnish

Spice Paste:
4 cloves garlic, peeled and sliced
8 red chilies, seeded and sliced
2 inches *kencur*, peeled and sliced
1 teaspoon dried shrimp paste (*trasi*), toasted
1 tablespoon tamarind juice
4 tablespoons chopped palm sugar
2 teaspoons salt

Arrange vegetables in a bowl. Grind or blend the **spice paste** ingredients together, adding a little water if necessary. Pour sauce over vegetables. Mix well and garnish with fried shallots and *krupuk*.

Opposite:
Karedok (right) and Lotek (left).

LOTEK

The sauce served with this cooked vegetable salad has ground peanuts for extra flavor and nutrition. It is said that Sundanese women have beautiful skin because they eat so many vegetables. ⏱ ⏱

8 ounces water spinach (*kangkung*) or regular spinach, steamed (about 5 cups)
8 ounces pumpkin or chayote, cut in chunks and steamed (about 2 cups)
8 ounces long beans, cut in 1 1/2-inch lengths and steamed (about 2 cups)
8 ounces young jackfruit, cubed and simmered in water until tender (about 2 cups)
1 cup bean sprouts, blanched
1 large potato, boiled, peeled and diced
5 bird's-eye chilies, sliced
3/4 inch *kencur*, sliced
1/2 teaspoon dried shrimp paste, toasted
1 teaspoon chopped palm sugar
1/4 teaspoon salt
1/2 cup fried peanuts, ground

Prepare the vegetables and set aside. Grind or blend the chilies, *kencur*, shrimp paste, palm sugar and salt. Mix well to make a sauce. Adjust seasonings to taste. Serve vegetables with sauce poured over and sprinkle with the ground fried peanuts.

GADO GADO & REMPEYEK KACANG

Vegetable Salad with Peanut Sauce & Crisp Peanut Wafers

*Opposite:
Rempeyek
Kacang (top left)
and Gado Gado
(center).*

GADO GADO 🕐

1 cup long beans, cut and blanched
1 cup bean sprouts, blanched
2 cups spinach, blanched
$^1/_4$ small cabbage, chopped and blanched
1 medium-sized carrot, thinly sliced and blanched
4 squares hard bean curd, deep fried and sliced
4 hard-boiled eggs, cut in wedges
2 tablespoons fried shallots

Peanut Sauce:

3 cups deep-fried peanuts
4 cloves garlic, peeled
10 bird's-eye chilies, sliced
3 inches *kencur*, peeled and chopped
3 kaffir lime leaves
$^1/_2$ cup sweet soy sauce
2 teaspoons salt
6 cups water
3 tablespoons fried shallots
1 tablespoon lime juice

Prepare the **sauce** by blending first 4 ingredients until coarse. Put in pan with all other ingredients, except fried shallots and lime juice. Simmer over very low heat for 1 hour, stirring to prevent sticking. Stir in lime juice and shallots just before use.

Arrange all vegetables on a dish and pour over the sauce. Garnish with bean curd and eggs, sprinkle with shallots and serve with deep-fried *krupuk*.

REMPEYEK KACANG 🕐🕐

$1^1/_4$ cups raw peanuts
14 tablespoons rice flour
$^3/_4$ cup white flour
1 cup coconut milk
Oil for deep frying

Spice Paste:

1 teaspoon coriander seeds
2 candlenuts
2 cloves garlic
$^1/_2$ inch fresh turmeric, peeled and sliced
   (or $^1/_2$ teaspoon powder)
5 kaffir lime leaves, shredded (optional)
1 teaspoon salt

Dry fry the peanuts in a wok over low heat for 5 minutes. Rub to remove the skin and set aside. Grind or blend the **spice paste** ingredients, then add to flours. Mix well, stirring in the coconut milk to blend well. Add the peanuts.

Heat plenty of oil in a wok and drop in a tablespoonful of batter at a time, cooking until golden brown. Drain and cool thoroughly before storing.

MARTABAK
Indian Savory Pancake

This Indian Muslim speciality, a night-time favorite, is often bought as a snack or light meal from food stalls. This recipe is sufficient to make 4 Martabak. ◔◔

2 tablespoons oil
4 cloves garlic, peeled and sliced
10 ounces minced or ground beef
7 ounces minced or ground lamb
1 medium-sized onion, halved and sliced
1 small leek, halved lengthwise and sliced
1 red chili, seeded and sliced
2 tablespoons chopped Chinese celery leaves
1 tablespoon curry powder
4 eggs
1 spring onion, finely sliced
Salt and white pepper to taste

Dough:
2 cups white flour
3 tablespoons oil
$^{3}/_{4}$ cup water
Pinch of salt

Prepare the **dough** first by combining all ingredients and kneading them into an oily elastic dough. Cover and leave at room temperature for 2 hours. Divide into 4 and roll each piece into a ball. Pull out with lightly oiled hands on an oiled or marble surface to make a large thin circle.

While dough is resting, make the filling. Heat oil and sauté garlic for a few seconds. Add minced meat and sauté over high heat until the meat changes color. Add onion, leek, chili and celery leaf and continue sautéing for another 2 minutes. Add curry powder, mix well and cook another 3 minutes. Set aside to cool.

To finish the Martabak, divide the cooked filling among 4 bowls. Add 1 egg, a little spring onion, salt and pepper to each and mix well. Heat a heavy frying pan or griddle. When it is hot, fill the center of each circle of dough with the mixture, fold in the sides and ends to completely enclose the filling envelope fashion.

Fry on the griddle until golden brown on one side, turn and fry the other side. Cut into pieces and serve, if desired, with vegetable pickles and sliced chilies.

DAGING BELACANG

Beef Soup with Chilies and Tamarind

An excellent way of dealing with tough cuts of beef, this soup from Timor in eastern Indonesia has a sweet-sour edge to it. ◍◍

2 pounds top round beef, in 1 piece
8 cups water
3 tablespoons oil
5 shallots, peeled and sliced
1 clove garlic, peeled and sliced
$\frac{1}{2}$ teaspoon dried shrimp paste (*trasi*), toasted
$\frac{3}{4}$ tablespoon chopped palm sugar
1 teaspoon sweet soy sauce
1 tablespoon tamarind juice
Salt to taste
2 red chilies, seeded and sliced in fine strips
2 spring onions, cut in 1-inch lengths

Simmer the meat in the water until half cooked, then cut in $\frac{3}{4}$-inch cubes, reserving the stock. Sauté beef in 2 tablespoons oil, then set aside.

Grind or blend the shallots, garlic, shrimp paste and palm sugar, then sauté in 1 tablespoon oil until fragrant. Add fried meat and sweet soy sauce and sauté for a couple of minutes. Add reserved beef stock, tamarind juice and salt and simmer until the beef is tender. Garnish with chilies and spring onions.

SOTO BANJAR

Chicken Soup with Eggs

Soto is a robust soupy dish given extra substance by noodles, Lontong (compressed rice) or potato croquettes (*pergedel*). If desired, the croquettes can be omitted and the dish garnished with potato chips. Most *soto* dishes originate in Java, but this version comes from Kalimantan. ☺ ☺ ☺

1 chicken weighing about 3 pounds
12 cups water
1 tablespoon oil
5 shallots, peeled and sliced
5 cloves garlic, peeled and sliced
10 bird's-eye chilies, sliced
3 kaffir lime leaves
2 sprigs Chinese celery, sliced
Salt and pepper to taste
5 hard-boiled eggs, peeled and quartered
2 tablespoons chopped Chinese celery leaf
Fried shallots to garnish

Potato Croquettes:

2 medium-sized potatoes, boiled, peeled and mashed
2 tablespoons fried shallots
$1/4$ teaspoon ground white pepper
1 spring onion, finely sliced
$1/2$ teaspoon salt
Little freshly grated nutmeg
1 tablespoon chopped Chinese celery leaf
Oil for deep frying
1 egg, beaten

Simmer chicken in water until tender. Leave chicken to cool in the stock, then remove, setting stock aside. Separate chicken meat from the bones and shred finely.

While chicken is simmering, make the **potato croquettes** by combining mashed potatoes with all other ingredients, except the oil and egg. Shape into flat patties and chill in refrigerator. Heat oil for deep frying. Dip each croquette in egg and deep fry until golden brown. Set aside.

Heat oil in heavy stockpot and sauté shallots, garlic and chilies over low heat for 5 minutes. Add 8 cups of the reserved chicken stock, lime leaves and sprigs of celery. Bring to a boil and simmer for 15 minutes. Season to taste with salt and pepper.

To serve, put the Soto into individual soup bowls. Add some of the shredded chicken and hard-boiled eggs, top with the potato croquettes and garnish with chopped celery leaf and fried shallots. Serve with Sambal Soto, if desired (page 45).

Helpful hint: Both the chicken stock and potato croquettes can be prepared well in advance, and everything reheated just before serving.

KONRO MAKASAR

Spicy Sparerib Soup

The Makasarese of Southern Sulawesi are renown-ed for their hearty beef soups. ⏱⏱⏱

2 pounds beef spareribs, cut in 2-inch lengths
16 cups water
4 shallots, peeled and sliced
2 cloves garlic, peeled and sliced
3 candlenuts
3 cups freshly grated or dried unsweetened
  coconut, fried until golden, then pounded
5 stalks lemongrass, bruised and tied
1 inch galangal (*laos*), peeled and sliced
3 kaffir lime leaves
$\frac{1}{2}$ teaspoon white peppercorns, crushed
1 teaspoon salt
1 tablespoon fried shallots
2 tablespoons sliced Chinese celery leaves

Put the beef ribs and water in a large pan and simmer, uncovered, until beef is tender.

Grind or blend the shallots, garlic, candlenuts and add to the pounded coconut. Put into the stock together with all remaining ingredients, except fried shallots and celery leaves. Simmer until the meat is very tender, but not falling from the bones. Serve garnished with fried shallots and celery.

SOP KEPALA IKAN
Fish-head Soup

This dish can be made with either one large fish head or a couple of smaller heads. There is not much flesh on the head, which is used to flavor the soup rather than to provide a substantial meal in itself. This version, which comes from West Sumatra, is eaten as an accompaniment to rice and other dishes. ◷◷

    4 cups water
    1 teaspoon salt
    3 stalks lemongrass, bruised
    5 kaffir lime leaves
    1 pound snapper heads, cleaned and well
        rinsed
    1 tablespoon fried shallots

Spice Paste:
    7 red chilies, seeded and sliced
    6 shallots, peeled and chopped
    3 cloves garlic, peeled and chopped
    2 inches ginger root, peeled and chopped
    1½ inches fresh turmeric, peeled and sliced
        (or 1½ teaspoons powder)
    1 tablespoon oil

Prepare the **spice paste** by grinding or blending all ingredients except oil, then sauté in oil for 2–3 minutes. Add water, salt, lemongrass and lime leaves and bring to a boil. Put in the fish heads, return to a boil and then simmer, uncovered, until the fish heads are cooked. Serve garnished with fried shallots.

NASI KUNING & NASI JAGUNG
Yellow Rice & Corn Rice

NASI KUNING

Rice colored with turmeric and shaped into a cone is often present on festive occasions. The shape echoes that of the mythical Hindu mountain, Meru, while yellow is the color of royalty and one of the four sacred colors for Balinese Hindus. ⏱

Opposite:
Nasi Kuning. The photograph of Nasi Jagung appears with Hagape Daging on page 108.

1$^1/_2$ cups uncooked long-grain rice, washed
   thoroughly
2 inches fresh turmeric, peeled and scraped
1$^1/_2$ cups coconut milk
$^1/_2$ cup chicken stock
1 *salam* leaf
1 pandan leaf, tied in a knot
1 stalk lemongrass, bruised
$^3/_4$ inch galangal (*laos*), peeled and sliced
2 teaspoons salt

Drain the rice in a sieve or colander. Put the fresh turmeric in a blender with $^1/_4$ cup water and process until fine. Strain through a sieve, pushing to extract all the juice. Measure 2 tablespoons and discard the rest. If fresh turmeric is not available, mix 2 teaspoons turmeric powder with 2 tablespoons water.

Put rice, turmeric water and all other ingredients in a heavy saucepan. Cover and bring to a boil over moderate heat. Stir, lower heat to the minimum and cook until the rice is done. Remove all leaves and galangal before serving, pressed into a cone shape, if desired.

Helpful hint: If the rice seems to be too dry before the grains are soft and swollen, sprinkle with a little more hot chicken stock and continue cooking.

NASI JAGUNG

Corn is often used to add bulk to rice in areas where rice is difficult to obtain or costly. Dried corn needs to be soaked for 24 hours before using, although this is obviously unnecessary if using fresh or canned sweet corn. ⏱

1$^1/_2$ cups uncooked rice, washed thoroughly
1$^1/_2$ cups sweet corn kernels, cut from raw corn
   cobs or canned

Put the rice and raw sweet corn in a pot with 3$^1/_2$ cups of water and bring to a boil. (If using canned sweet corn, do not add at this stage.) Simmer the rice and corn until the water is absorbed. If using canned sweet corn, add now. Lower heat to the minimum and cook rice and corn for another 10 minutes, until the rice is dry and fluffy.

NASI GORENG
Fried Rice

One of Indonesia's best-known dishes and found throughout the archipelago, Nasi Goreng is prepared in countless ways, depending upon the availability of ingredients and the cook's inclination. This is a basic version, which can be accompanied by a fried egg, fried chicken, satay and shrimp crackers (*krupuk*) for a substantial meal. If the fried rice is to be served without substantial accompaniments, you can add pieces of chicken, pork or shrimp, as well as a little shredded cabbage, to the rice during cooking. ⏱

   4 cups cold cooked rice
   2 tablespoons oil
   1 egg, lightly beaten
   5 shallots, peeled and sliced
   2 cloves garlic, peeled and sliced
   3 red chilies, sliced
   1 teaspoon dried shrimp paste (*trasi*)
   ¹/₂ teaspoon salt
   1 tablespoon sweet soy sauce
   Sliced cucumber and sliced tomato to garnish

Stir the rice with a fork to separate the grains. Lightly grease a nonstick pan with a few drops of oil and fry the egg to make a thin omelet. Cool, then shred.

Heat remaining oil in a wok and fry the shallots, garlic, chilies and shrimp paste until soft. (If using other ingredients such as shrimp and chicken, add now and stir fry until cooked.)

Increase the heat to maximum and add the rice, salt and soy sauce, stirring constantly until well mixed and heated through. Serve garnished with the shredded omelet, cucumber and tomato. Accompany, if desired, with a fried egg, fried chicken, satay and *krupuk*.

Helpful hint: It is essential that the rice is cold, otherwise the grains will be too soft and absorb the oil. In Asia, rice left overnight is preferred for any fried rice dish as it is thoroughly dry.

NASI KEBULI

Chicken Rice with Pineapple

Middle Eastern and Indian Muslim influences are evident in this all-in-one rice meal from Northern Sumatra. ⏱ ⏱

2 tablespoons butter or oil
1 pound boneless chicken, cut in
  $\frac{1}{2}$-inch cubes
3 cups chicken stock
1 teaspoon salt
2 cups uncooked long-grain rice, washed and drained
$\frac{1}{2}$ small pineapple, peeled and sliced and cut in small pieces

Seasoning:

13 shallots, peeled and finely chopped
7 cloves garlic, peeled and finely chopped
1 inch ginger root, peeled and chopped
1 teaspoon coriander seeds
$\frac{1}{2}$ teaspoon white peppercorns
$\frac{1}{2}$ teaspoon cumin seeds
A little freshly grated nutmeg
3 inches cinnamon stick
4 cardamom pods, bruised
2 cloves
1 stalk lemongrass, bruised

Heat butter or oil in wok or heavy saucepan, add all **seasoning** ingredients and sauté for 2–3 minutes. Add the chicken and continue sautéing for 3 minutes over high heat.

Add chicken stock and salt and simmer until chicken is tender. Strain the stock and set aside the chicken pieces. Place rice in a rice cooker or heavy stockpot, add $2\frac{1}{2}$ cups of the reserved chicken stock and bring to a boil. Cover the pan and simmer until the rice is almost cooked and the liquid absorbed. Add the diced chicken and cook over low heat until the rice is thoroughly cooked.

Serve on a platter garnished with fried shallots and pineapple pieces.

GULAI TEMPEH & SAMBAL GORENG TEMPEH
Tempeh Stew & Hot Spicy Fried Tempeh

GULAI TEMPEH

A Sumatran dish using protein-rich *tempeh*, this is unusual (for Sumatra) in it's absence of chilies. Any leafy green vegetable, such as spinach or water spinach (*kangkung*), can be substituted for tapioca (cassava) leaves. ◑ ◑

Opposite:
*Gulai Tempeh
(left) and Sambal
Goreng Tempeh
(right).*

2 cups coconut milk
2 whole cloves
4 fermented soy bean cakes (*tempeh*),
  cut in cubes
1 bunch (about 8 ounces) tapioca leaves
  or substitute
Salt to taste
Fried shallots to garnish

Spice Paste:

4 cloves garlic, peeled and sliced
1 teaspoon white peppercorns, crushed
1 inch ginger root, peeled and sliced
1½ inches fresh turmeric, peeled and sliced
  (or 1½ teaspoons powder)
1 tablespoon chopped palm sugar

Prepare the **spice paste** by grinding or blending all ingredients. Bring coconut milk to a boil, then add the spice paste, cloves, *tempeh* and tapioca leaves. Simmer, uncovered, until tender and the sauce has thickened. Season to taste with salt and garnish with fried shallots.

SAMBAL GORENG TEMPEH

Sweet with palm sugar and tangy with chilies, this is a Javanese favorite, which is served with rice and other dishes. ◑ ◑

2 fermented soy bean cakes (*tempeh*), cut in
  long narrow strips and deep fried
1 tablespoon oil
2 shallots, peeled and sliced
3 cloves garlic, sliced
2 red chilies, sliced
1 inch galangal (*laos*), peeled and sliced
½ teaspoon dried shrimp paste (*trasi*)
5 tablespoons chopped palm sugar
3 tablespoons water
1 tablespoon tamarind juice
Salt to taste
8 bird's-eye chilies, chopped

Prepare the *tempeh* and set aside. Heat the oil and sauté the shallots, garlic, chilies, galangal and shrimp paste for 2–3 minutes. Add the palm sugar, water and tamarind juice and stir until the sugar has dissolved. Put in the *tempeh* and cook, stirring frequently, until the sauce has reduced and caramelized. Season to taste with salt. Add the bird's-eye chilies just before serving.

GULAI RAMPON & PELECING KANGKUNG

Vegetables in Coconut Milk & Water Spinach with Spicy Sauce

GULAI RAMPON ⏱⏱

2 cups coconut milk
1½ cups each of tapioca (cassava) leaves, sweet potato leaves, spinach and *melinjo* leaves
½ cup chopped long beans
1 fresh or frozen corn cob, cut in thick slices
Small shrimp, peeled and deveined
½ cup fresh *melinjo* nuts or ½ cup lightly boiled peanuts
Salt to taste

Spice Paste:

3 shallots, peeled and sliced
3 green chilies, seeded and sliced
4 bird's-eye chilies, sliced
4–6 sour carambola fruit (*belimbing wuluh*) or 2 tablespoons tamarind juice
1 medium-sized tomato, skinned and sliced
½ teaspoon salt

Grind or blend all **spice paste** ingredients together to a coarse paste. Bring coconut milk to a boil, stirring, then add spice paste and simmer, uncovered, for 2 minutes. Add all the vegetables, shrimp and nuts, then simmer, uncovered, until the vegetables are tender and the sauce has thickened. Season with salt and serve with rice and other dishes.

Opposite:
Gulai Rampon (top) and Pelecing Kangkung (bottom).

PELECING KANGKUNG ⏱⏱

1 pound water spinach, steamed
1 tomato, blackened over a grill and peeled
6 bird's-eye chilies, sliced
½ teaspoon dried shrimp paste, toasted
1 teaspoon salt
1 teaspoon lime juice
2 tablespoons warm water
1 cup freshly grated coconut
1 clove garlic
1 kaffir lime leaf, finely shredded
1 teaspoon chopped palm sugar
2 tablespoons fried peanuts

Cut steamed vegetable in 2-inch lengths. Grind together the tomato, chilies, shrimp paste and salt, then mix with lime juice and water. Set aside.

Grind the coconut, garlic, lime leaf and palm sugar together until fine. Just before serving, toss the vegetable with the tomato and lime juice mixture and put on a plate. Sprinkle with the grated coconut mixture and garnish with peanuts.

Helpful hint: If water spinach is not available, substitute another leafy green.

PACRI NENAS & JANGAN OLAH

Spiced Pineapple Stew & Vegetables with Spicy Coconut

Opposite:
*Pacri Nanas (top)
and Jangan
Olah (bottom).*

PACRI NENAS ⏱⏱

3$\frac{1}{2}$ cups coconut milk
1 just-ripe pineapple, peeled and cubed
$\frac{1}{4}$ teaspoon black peppercorns
2 whole star anise
3 inches stick cinnamon
2 cloves
A little freshly grated nutmeg
1 stalk lemongrass, bruised
1 inch galangal (*laos*), peeled and sliced
1 tablespoon tamarind juice
Salt to taste
$\frac{1}{2}$ cup thick coconut milk
Fried shallots to garnish

Spice Paste:

5 dried red chilies, soaked to soften
1 teaspoon coriander seeds, crushed
2 cloves garlic, peeled and chopped
6 shallots, peeled and chopped
2 candlenuts
$\frac{1}{2}$ inch fresh turmeric, peeled and sliced
$\frac{1}{2}$ teaspoon chopped palm sugar
2 tablespoons oil

Grind or blend **spice paste**. Heat oil and sauté until fragrant, then add 3$\frac{1}{2}$ cups coconut milk. Bring to a boil, stirring, then add all other ingredients, except thick coconut milk and shallots. Simmer until the pineapple is tender. Add thick coconut milk and heat through. Garnish with fried shallots.

JANGAN OLAH ⏱⏱

2 cups chopped long beans
2 cups young fern tips (fiddleheads) or
  chopped spinach
1 cup bean sprouts, blanched
Fried shallots to garnish

Sauce:

7 bird's-eye chilies, sliced
8 red chilies, seeded and sliced
1 tablespoon dried shrimp paste (*trasi*), toasted
4 cloves garlic, peeled and sliced
4 shallots, peeled and sliced
1 inch fresh turmeric, peeled and sliced
  (or 1 teaspoon powder)
1 tablespoon chopped palm sugar
3 cups freshly grated or dried unsweetened
  coconut
4 cups water
3 *salam* leaves
Salt to taste

Prepare **sauce** first by grinding or blending first 7 ingredients. Simmer with remaining ingredients until the sauce thickens. Cool to room temperature.

Lightly boil or steam the long beans and fern tips or spinach. Drain thoroughly and arrange on a plate. Add blanched bean sprouts. Serve vegetables with sauce poured over and garnished with fried shallots.

ASAM-ASAM TERONG & GULAI DAUN PAKIS
Stewed Eggplant & Fern Tips in Coconut Milk

ASAM-ASAM TERONG

A quickly prepared vegetable dish that enhances the rather bland flavor of eggplant. In Indonesia, the most common variety of eggplant is long and slim (about 6–8 inches). They lack the bitterness of their large European counterpart and do not need salting before use. 🕐🕐

2 cups water
4 red chilies, seeded and sliced
3 shallots, peeled and sliced
2 cloves garlic, peeled and sliced
1½ pounds eggplant, halved lengthwise
  (or sliced if using large European variety)
1 medium-sized tomato, sliced
½ teaspoon chopped palm sugar
Salt

Garnish:
Fried shallots
3 sprigs Chinese celery leaf, chopped
Spring onions, sliced

Combine water, chilies, shallots and garlic and simmer, uncovered, for 5 minutes. Add the eggplant and continue simmering until half cooked. Then add the tomato and sugar and simmer until the vegetable is soft. Season to taste with salt and garnish with fried shallots, celery and spring onions.

GULAI DAUN PAKIS

The young tips of several varieties of wild fern are enjoyed in many parts of Indonesia. They can often be found in markets throughout Southeast Asia and have an excellent flavor. If you are unable to find fern tips (fiddleheads), spinach is an acceptable substitute or, if you're feeling extravagant, you could use fresh asparagus. 🕐🕐

3 cups coconut milk
1 pound fern tips (or fiddleheads), cleaned
2 turmeric leaves (optional)
1 tablespoon tamarind juice
Salt to taste

Spice Paste:
3 shallots, peeled and sliced
2 cloves garlic, peeled and sliced
10 red chilies, seeded and sliced
1 inch galangal (*laos*), peeled and sliced
1 inch fresh turmeric (or 1 teaspoon powder),
  peeled and sliced
1 inch ginger root, peeled and sliced

Prepare **spice paste** by grinding or blending all ingredients together. Put spice paste in a saucepan with the coconut milk and bring to a boil, stirring. Simmer for 1 minute, then add the fern tips, turmeric leaves and tamarind juice. Simmer, stirring frequently, until the fern tips are tender. Season to taste with salt.

SAMBAL UDANG

Shrimp in Hot Sauce

The distinctive and somewhat bitter flavor of twisted cluster beans (*petai*) is an excellent counterpart to the shrimp in this spicy dish. Even if *petai* are not available, the shrimp partnered with potatoes and a rich sauce are excellent. 🕐 🕐

- 1 pound shrimp
- 5 pods (about 20 beans) twisted cluster beans (*petai*), optional
- 2 cups coconut milk
- 4 potatoes, peeled and cut in wedges
- 1 tablespoon tamarind juice
- 1 teaspoon salt

Spice Paste:
- 5 shallots
- 2 cloves garlic
- 5 red chilies, sliced
- $\frac{1}{2}$ teaspoon dried shrimp paste
- 2 tablespoons oil

Peel the shrimp and devein. Open the pods and remove the beans.

Prepare the **spice paste** by grinding or pounding all ingredients, except oil. Heat oil and sauté the spice paste until fragrant.

Add the shrimp and sauté until they change color. Put in the beans and coconut milk and bring to a boil, stirring. Add the potatoes and tamarind juice and simmer, uncovered, until potatoes and shrimp are cooked and the sauce has thickened. Season with salt and serve.

UDANG PANTUNG KUNING

Lobster in Yellow Sauce

A real gourmet treat from Bali, this could also be made with huge shrimp. In Bali, coconut chunks are roasted directly on charcoal, then the charred skin scraped off and the flesh grated for making the coconut milk. ⊘ ⊘

4 small lobsters, weighing about 1 pound each, or 2 pounds large shrimp
5 cups water
2 stalks lemongrass, bruised
2 fragrant lime leaves
Few drops white vinegar
4 cups coconut milk
Fried shallots to garnish

Spice Paste:

5 red chilies, seeded and chopped
3 cloves garlic, peeled and chopped
7 shallots, peeled and chopped
2 inches fresh turmeric, peeled and chopped (or 2 teaspoons powder)
2 inches ginger root, peeled and chopped
5 candlenuts
$1^{1}/_{2}$ teaspoons coriander seeds
$^{1}/_{2}$ teaspoon dried shrimp paste (*trasi*), toasted
1 small tomato, peeled and seeded
2 tablespoons oil
$1^{1}/_{2}$ tablespoons tamarind pulp
1 *salam* leaf
1 stalk lemongrass, bruised

Prepare **spice paste** by grinding or blending all ingredients except oil, tamarind, *salam* leaf and lemongrass. Heat oil, add spice paste and all other ingredients. Cook over moderate heat for about 5 minutes, then cool.

Wash lobsters and leave whole. Bring water to a boil, add lobsters and simmer for 15 minutes. Remove lobsters, plunge in iced water for 1 minute, then drain and remove meat. Return shells to the pot of water, keeping lobster meat aside.

Add spice paste, lemongrass, lime leaves and vinegar to the water with the shells and simmer until 4 cups of stock remain. Add coconut milk and simmer for 10 minutes. Strain stock and return to pan. Add lobster and simmer for 1 minute. Serve garnished with fried shallots and accompanied by white rice.

Helpful hint: If using shrimp instead of lobster, peel the raw shrimp and put the shells in 4 cups of water. Simmer for 5 minutes, then combine this stock with coconut milk, shrimp and all other ingredients, simmering until cooked.

OTAK OTAK & OTAK OTAK PIPIH

Grilled Fish in Banana Leaf & Fried Fish Cakes

Opposite:
Roasted Otak
Otak (top) and
deep-fried Otak
Otak Pipih (right).

OTAK OTAK

This Kalimantan recipe calls for steamed bundles of minced, seasoned fish to be cooked directly on hot charcoal, giving an inimitable flavor. ☉ ☉

1¼ pounds boneless white fish fillets
   (such as snapper), skinned and chopped
15 shallots, peeled and sliced
3 garlic cloves, peeled and sliced
3 spring onions, chopped
1 teaspoon white peppercorns, crushed
½ cup thick coconut milk
1 tablespoon lime juice
1 teaspoon salt
3 eggs
Pieces of banana leaf or aluminum foil,
   5 inches square, for wrapping

Put fish in a blender and process for a few seconds. Add all other ingredients, except for banana leaf, and process until well blended.

Put 3 heaped tablespoons of fish in the center of each square of banana leaf and wrap as directed on the bottom of page 31. Steam the parcels for 15 minutes, then place directly onto charcoal or under a broiler for 5 minutes, turning from time to time, until the leaves are charred.

Serve still wrapped in banana leaf.

OTAK OTAK PIPIH

These Javanese fish cakes are well flavored and have the added advantage of being able to be prepared several hours in advance, provided they are refrigerated, before the final deep frying. Spanish mackerel, snapper, or any other white fish can be used. ☉ ☉

1¼ pounds boneless white fish fillets, skinned
1 teaspoon sugar
1 teaspoon salt
2 eggs
1 cup freshly grated or dried unsweetened
   coconut, fried until golden
1 cup thick coconut milk
Oil for deep frying

Spice Paste:

3 shallots, peeled and chopped
2 cloves garlic, peeled and chopped
2 candlenuts, chopped
½ inch galangal (*laos*), peeled and chopped
½ inch ginger root, peeled and chopped

Grind or blend the **spice paste** ingredients finely. Add the fish and process until fine, then put into a large bowl and stir in all other ingredients, except oil. Shape the mixture into cakes and deep fry in hot oil until cooked and golden brown.

ARSIN IKAN MAS

Simmered River Fish

With its plentiful lakes and rivers, Sumatra is the source for many delicious freshwater fish recipes, including this one. ⏱⏱

1½ pounds freshwater fish, either 1 large fish or 2–4 smaller fish, cleaned and gutted
½ teaspoon salt
Liberal sprinkle of ground white pepper
2 cups water
2 stalks lemongrass, bruised
2 tablespoons tamarind juice

Spice Paste:

8 shallots, peeled and chopped
3 cloves garlic, peeled and chopped
½ teaspoon salt
6 candlenuts
1 inch ginger root, peeled and sliced
1 inch fresh turmeric, peeled and sliced (or 1 teaspoon powder)
1 inch galangal (*laos*), peeled and sliced
15 red chilies, seeded and sliced

Garnish:

3 spring onions, chopped
½ small pineapple, peeled and sliced
2 fresh limes or lemons, cut in wedges

Season fish inside and outside with salt and pepper. Prepare the **spice paste** by grinding or blending all ingredients finely. Put in a pan with the water and all other ingredients, except fish. Bring to a boil, reduce heat and simmer, uncovered, for 10 minutes. Add a little more water if the stock evaporates too much.

Add fish and continue to simmer until cooked, turning fish over gently from time to time. Remove fish carefully from stock, arrange on platter and pour stock over. Garnish with spring onions, pineapple and lime.

IKAN BUMBU ACAR

Spicy Fried Sardines

Small fresh fish, such as sardines, are used in this typical seafood dish from the fishing villages near Pekalongan, on the northern coast of Central Java. ⏲⏲

1¼ pounds sardines or other small fish,
    cleaned
2 teaspoons salt
6 tablespoons oil
2 red chilies, seeded and sliced
13 green bird's-eye chilies, sliced
2 cloves garlic, peeled and sliced
7 shallots, peeled and sliced
½ inch ginger root, peeled and sliced
½ inch galangal, peeled and sliced
1 large tomato, cut in wedges
2 tablespoons tamarind juice
1 *salam* leaf
½ teaspoon brown sugar
3 tablespoons water
Basil sprigs to garnish (optional)

Spice Paste:

1 inch fresh turmeric, peeled and chopped
    (or 1 teaspoon powder)
½ inch ginger root, peeled and chopped
2 candlenuts
2 shallots, peeled and sliced
2 cloves garlic, peeled and chopped
1 teaspoon white peppercorns, crushed
½ teaspoon coriander seeds, crushed
2 tablespoons vegetable oil

Prepare **spice paste** by grinding or blending all ingredients, except oil. Heat oil and gently sauté the spice paste for 3–5 minutes until fragrant, then set aside.

Wash the sardines, drain and sprinkle with salt. Heat 3 tablespoons of the oil in a wok and sauté the chilies, garlic, shallots, ginger, galangal, tomato, tamarind juice and *salam* leaf over high heat for 1 minute, stirring constantly. Add sugar, then the spice paste and fry for another 2 minutes, stirring frequently.

In another pan, heat remaining oil and fry the fish until golden brown. Drain, then combine with the spicy sauce in the wok and add water. Cook for another minute, stirring to mix well, then serve garnished with basil.

IKAN BAKAR COLO COLO
Grilled Fish with Tomato Sambal

Fish, grilled plain or wrapped in banana leaf, is very popular in both Sulawesi and Maluku. This recipe from Maluku is very simple, the flavor coming from the Colo Colo Sambal. ⏱

1 whole fish, approximately 2 pounds, cleaned
$\frac{1}{4}$ teaspoon salt
1 tablespoon lime juice
2 tablespoons oil
Large piece of banana leaf or aluminum foil
    to wrap fish

Colo Colo Sambal:

3 tablespoons lime or lemon juice
2 tomatoes, cut in half and sliced
5 red chilies, seeded and sliced
4 shallots, peeled and sliced
4 tablespoons light soy sauce
4 sprigs basil, chopped

Season fish with salt and lime juice, then brush with oil. Wrap fish into banana leaf and place parcel directly on charcoal or under a grill. Cook until banana leaves are evenly browned and fish is done.

To make the **Colo Colo Sambal**, combine all ingredients and mix well. The sauce can be poured over the fish when serving or, as is usually the case in Indonesia, put into individual sauce bowls for each diner to add to the fish as desired.

TELUR PETIS & GULAI TELUR

Eggs in Fragrant Sauce & Padang-style Eggs in Coconut Milk

TELUR PETIS

Duck eggs are generally preferred for this emphatically flavored dish, although hen eggs can be substituted. 🕐🕐

4 cups coconut milk
4 bird's-eye chilies, bruised
3 stalks lemongrass, bruised
3 *salam* leaves
1 tablespoon black shrimp paste (*petis*)
8 duck or hen eggs, hard-boiled and peeled
Salt to taste
Fried shallots to garnish

Spice Paste:

8 red chilies, seeded and chopped
6 shallots, peeled and chopped
4 cloves garlic, peeled and chopped
$\frac{1}{2}$ inch fresh turmeric, peeled and sliced
$\frac{1}{2}$ inch galangal (*laos*), peeled and sliced
$\frac{1}{2}$ teaspoon dried shrimp paste (*trasi*)
2 tablespoons oil
1 teaspoon brown sugar

Grind or blend the **spice paste** ingredients, except for oil and sugar, until fine. Heat oil and sauté spice paste for 3–5 minutes until it smells fragrant, then add sugar and sauté for 1 minute.

Add the coconut milk, chilies, lemongrass, *salam* leaves and black shrimp paste. Bring slowly to a boil, stirring, then add eggs and simmer until the sauce thickens. Season to taste with salt and garnish with fried shallots.

GULAI TELUR

A full-bodied dish often served at a typical West Sumatran or Padang-style meal. 🕐🕐

2 cups coconut milk
$\frac{1}{2}$ turmeric leaf, shredded (optional)
8 hard-boiled eggs, peeled
1 tablespoon tamarind juice
Salt to taste
Fried shallots to garnish

Spice Paste:

5 shallots, peeled and sliced
3 cloves garlic
4 bird's-eye chilies, chopped
1 inch ginger root, peeled and chopped
$\frac{1}{2}$ inch fresh turmeric, peeled and sliced
1 inch galangal (*laos*), peeled and chopped

Grind or blend **spice paste** ingredients until coarse. Bring coconut milk gradually to a boil and add the spice paste, turmeric leaf and eggs. Simmer until the sauce thickens, then add tamarind juice and salt and simmer for another minute. Serve garnished with fried shallots.

Opposite:
Telur Petis (right) and Gulai Telur (left).

AYAM TALIWANG

Chicken with Spicy Sauce

Lombok's most famous chicken dish is usually grilled over a charcoal fire and served with a spicy coconut-milk sauce. This version suggests partially grilling the chicken, finishing it off by deep frying. Alternatively, the chicken could be deep fried only, depending on your preference. ⏱

1 whole fresh chicken
1 teaspoon salt
Oil for deep frying

Sauce:

4 red chilies, seeded and sliced
8 bird's-eye chilies, seeded and sliced
4 shallots, peeled and sliced
1 teaspoon dried shrimp paste (*trasi*), toasted
1 teaspoon chopped palm sugar
1 teaspoon salt
2 tablespoons oil
4 cups coconut milk
1 tablespoon lime or lemon juice

Prepare the **sauce** by grinding or blending all ingredients, except oil, coconut milk and lime juice. Heat oil in a pan and sauté the ground paste for 2–3 minutes, then add the coconut milk and simmer, uncovered, until the sauce thickens. Add the lime juice and set sauce aside. If the sauce is prepared in advance, it can be reheated just before needed.

Slit the chicken open along the back and remove the backbone. Press with the hands to make a butterfly shape and fasten with a skewer to hold it flat. If preferred, the chicken can be cut into large serving pieces. Sprinkle the chicken with salt and grill over hot charcoal until half cooked.

Heat plenty of oil in a wok and fry the chicken until golden brown and crisp. Serve with the sauce.

AYAM CINCANE

Chicken with Green Tomatoes

This recipe comes from West and South Kaliman-tan, where it is usually made with a free-range or *kampung* chicken. As this is often as tough as it is flavorful, the meat is simmered in water first. If you are using a normal tender chicken, this pre-liminary step is very brief. ☻ ☻

1 fresh chicken (2$\frac{1}{2}$–3$\frac{1}{2}$ pounds), cut in 8–12 pieces
1 teaspoon salt
1 tablespoon lime or lemon juice
10 red chilies, seeded and sliced
12 shallots, peeled and sliced
4 green tomatoes, sliced
1 sprig basil
3 kaffir lime leaves
2 spring onions, sliced
$\frac{1}{2}$ inch ginger root, peeled and sliced
5 bird's-eye chilies, sliced

Season the chicken with salt and lime juice and set aside for 20 minutes. Put the chicken in a wok, add 2 cups of water and simmer, uncovered, until the chicken is just tender. Add all remaining ingre-dients, except bird's-eye chilies, and continue cook-ing for another 5 minutes.

Sprinkle with bird's-eye chilies and serve.

AYAM MASAK BUGIS
Buginese Chicken

A Buginese favorite from Southern Sulawesi, this simmers a whole chicken in seasoned stock and coconut milk. ☺ ☺

    1 whole chicken (2$\frac{1}{2}$–3$\frac{1}{2}$ pounds)
    4 cups chicken stock
    2 cloves garlic, peeled and sliced
    12 shallots, peeled and sliced
    1 tablespoon dried shrimp paste (*trasi*), toasted
    2 tablespoons tamarind juice
    2 teaspoons white peppercorns, crushed
    2 *salam* leaves
    3 inches cinnamon stick
    4 cloves
    $\frac{1}{4}$ teaspoon freshly grated nutmeg
    1 teaspoon salt
    1 teaspoon chopped palm sugar
    1 tablespoon white vinegar
    4 cups coconut milk
    Fried shallots to garnish

Leave chicken whole. Bring chicken stock to a boil in a heavy saucepan, then add all other ingredients, except chicken, coconut milk and fried shallots. Bring back to a boil, lower heat and simmer, uncovered, for 5 minutes.

Add the chicken and coconut milk. Bring back to a boil, stirring frequently, then lower heat. Simmer uncovered, turning chicken from time to time, until it is tender. Remove chicken and continue simmering the stock until reduced by half. Serve garnished with fried shallots, accompanied by white rice and mixed vegetables.

Helpful hint: Vegetables such as a few long beans, sweet corn kernels, spinach leaves and tomato can be added 5–10 minutes before the end of cooking time.

OPOR AYAM & AYAM GORENG YOGYA

Chicken in Coconut Milk & Yogya Fried Chicken

OPOR AYAM

A mild dish without chilies but redolent with the fragrance of lemongrass, *salam* leaves and galangal, Opor Ayam is a universal favorite. ⏱ ⏱

$^1/_2$ cup thick coconut milk
1 chicken ($2^3/_4$ pounds), cut in 8–12 pieces
3 cups regular coconut milk
1 stalk lemongrass, bruised
2 *salam* leaves
1 teaspoon salt

Spice Paste:

1 heaped tablespoon coriander seeds
2 teaspoons cumin seeds
1 teaspoon white peppercorns
2 shallots, peeled and sliced
3 cloves garlic, peeled and sliced
5 candlenuts
1 inch galangal (*laos*), peeled and sliced
$^1/_2$ tablespoon chopped palm sugar

Prepare **spice paste** by grinding the coriander, cumin and peppercorns to a powder, then add all other ingredients and blend finely. Simmer thick coconut milk and spice paste together until the milk is thick and oily, then add all other ingredients. Simmer gently, uncovered, until chicken is tender.

AYAM GORENG YOGYA

Seasoned chicken is simmered until almost cooked, then deep-fried to make this central Javanese favorite. ⏱ ⏱

1 fresh chicken ($2^3/_4$ pounds), cut in 8 pieces
2 cups water
Oil for deep frying

Spice Paste:

1 tablespoon coriander seeds
3 cloves garlic, peeled and sliced
$^3/_4$ inch fresh turmeric, peeled and sliced
$^3/_4$ inch ginger root, peeled and sliced
$^1/_2$ inch galangal (*laos*), peeled and sliced
1 tablespoon chopped palm sugar
2 tablespoons oil
2 *salam* leaves

Prepare the **spice paste** by grinding or blending all ingredients, except oil and *salam* leaves, until fine. Heat oil in a wok and sauté the spice paste and *salam* leaves for 3 minutes. Add chicken and cook, stirring, until well coated. Add water and simmer, uncovered, until chicken is almost cooked and sauce is dry. Leave to cool.

Just before chicken is required, heat oil and deep fry chicken until crisp and golden brown. Serve with the *sambal* of your choice.

Opposite:
Opor Ayam (top) and Ayam Goreng Yogya (bottom).

BEBEK MENYATNYAT
Duck Curry

Ducks waddling along the banks of the rice fields or following the flag held by their owner (or his children) are a common sight in Bali. On festive occasions, duck is a great favorite. Spiced stuffed duck baked in banana leaf is one popular recipe; this curry-like dish is another. Chicken could be used as a substitute for duck, if preferred. ⓓ ⓓ

    1 whole duck, weighing about 4¹/₂ pounds
    8 cups coconut milk
    2 stalks lemongrass, bruised
    2 *salam* leaves
    1 tablespoon salt
    1 teaspoon black peppercorns, crushed
    Fried shallots to garnish

Spice Paste:
    12 shallots, peeled and sliced
    6 cloves garlic, peeled and sliced
    4 red chilies, sliced
    1 inch galangal (*laos*), peeled and sliced
    1 inch *kencur*, peeled and sliced
    2 inches fresh turmeric, peeled and sliced
    2 teaspoons coriander seeds, crushed
    3 candlenuts
    1 teaspoon dried shrimp paste (*trasi*)
    ¹/₄ teaspoon black peppercorns, crushed
    Pinch of freshly grated nutmeg
    2 cloves
    3 tablespoons oil

Cut the duck into 12 pieces and pat dry.

Prepare the **spice paste** by grinding or blending all ingredients, except oil. Heat the oil and sauté the spice paste for 2 minutes. Add the duck, increase heat and sauté for 3 minutes, stirring frequently. Add the coconut milk and all other ingredients, except fried shallots, and simmer, uncovered, until the duck is tender and the sauce has thickened.

Garnish with fried shallots and serve with white rice.

SATE LILIT BEBEK & SATE SAPI
Minced Duck Satay & Beef Satay

SATE LILIT BEBEK ◷◷

1¼ pounds duck or chicken meat, minced
2 cups freshly grated coconut
5 kaffir lime leaves, very finely shredded
1 teaspoon black peppercorns, crushed
1 teaspoon salt
3–5 bird's-eye chilies, very finely chopped
2 tablespoons chopped palm sugar
Lemongrass or satay skewers

Spice Paste:

12 shallots, peeled and sliced
6 cloves garlic, peeled and sliced
3 red chilies, sliced
1 inch galangal (*laos*), peeled and sliced
1 inch *kencur*, peeled and sliced
2 inches fresh turmeric, peeled and sliced
2 teaspoons coriander seeds
½ teaspoon black peppercorns
3 candlenuts
1 teaspoon dried shrimp paste (*trasi*)
Pinch of freshly grated nutmeg
2 cloves
2 tablespoons oil

Grind or blend all **spice paste** ingredients, except oil. Heat oil and sauté spice paste for about 5 minutes. Cool, then combine with duck and all other ingredients except lemongrass. Mold about 2 tablespoonfuls on lemongrass or skewers and grill over hot charcoal until cooked and golden brown.

Opposite:
Sate Lilit Bebek (bottom) and Sate Sapi (top).

SATE SAPI ◷◷

1¼ pounds top round beef, in ½-inch cubes
3–5 bird's-eye chilies
2 tablespoons brown sugar

Spice Paste:

10 shallots, peeled and sliced
6 cloves garlic, peeled and sliced
4 inches galangal (*laos*), peeled and sliced
2 inches ginger root peeled and sliced
6 red chilies, sliced
7 bird's-eye chilies, sliced
10 candlenuts
1 tablespoon black peppercorns
1 tablespoon coriander seeds
4 tablespoons chopped palm sugar
2 *salam* leaves
4 tablespoons oil

Prepare **spice paste** by blending all ingredients, except *salam* leaves and oil. Sauté blended mixture in oil with *salam* leaves for 5 minutes until golden brown. Cool, then combine with meat, chilies and sugar. Marinate in the refrigerator for 24 hours (can be kept up to 4 days). Thread meat onto satay skewers and grill over high heat until cooked. Serve with peanut sauce or Sambal Kecap (page 44).

SATE AMPET SASAK & SATE MADURA
Mixed Beef Satay & Lamb Satay

SATE AMPET SASAK

In Lombok, as in neighboring Bali, the meat used for satay is usually highly seasoned before grilling. If beef heart is difficult to obtain, use about 1 pound each of top round and liver. ⏲ ⏲

> **10 ounces beef top round**
> **10 ounces beef heart**
> **10 ounces beef liver**
> **Lime or lemon wedges**

Marinade:

> **2 red chilies, seeded and sliced**
> **3 bird's-eye chilies**
> **5 cloves garlic, peeled and sliced**
> **1/2 teaspoon dried shrimp paste (*trasi*)**
> **4 candlenuts**
> **1 inch ginger root, peeled and sliced**
> **1/4 teaspoon salt**
> **3 tablespoons oil**
> **2 cups coconut milk**

Prepare **marinade** by grinding or blending all ingredients, except oil and coconut milk. Heat oil and sauté the mixture until it turns golden and smells fragrant, then add the coconut milk and simmer until thickened. Divide among four bowls.

Opposite: Sate Ampet Sasak (left) and Sate Madura (right).

Cut each of the meats into squares of about 3/4 inch and marinate separately in three of the bowls for a minimum of 2 hours. Remove meats and discard marinade. Thread the meat onto satay skewers and grill until cooked. Serve with the remaining marinade as a dipping sauce, accompanied by lime wedges.

SATE MADURA

Normally made with goat, this is the most common satay in Indonesia, originating in the island of Madura just to the northeast of Java. ⏲

> **2 pounds leg of lamb, cut in 3/4-inch cubes**
> **1/2 cup sweet soy sauce**
> **1/2 teaspoon coriander seeds, crushed**
> **1/4 teaspoon white peppercorns, crushed**
> **1 tablespoon lime or lemon juice**
> **4 shallots, peeled and sliced**

Thread the lamb cubes onto satay skewers. Combine all other ingredients except for shallots, mixing well. Spoon some of the sauce over each skewer to cover meat well. Drain, then grill the satay over hot charcoal. Combine the remaining sauce with shallots and serve as a dip for the cooked satay.

BABI MASAK TOMAT & TINARANSAY

Pork Cooked with Tomatoes & Ginger Pork

BABI MASAK TOMAT

A simple recipe from Kalimantan, where pork (particularly wild boar from the jungle) is popular among the Dyaks. 🕐

- 1 pound pork, cut in $^3/_4$-inch cubes
- 4 tomatoes, sliced
- 4–6 coarse chives (*kucai*), or spring onions
- 1 stalk lemongrass, bruised
- 1 cup water

Spice Paste:

- 4 shallots, peeled and sliced
- 4 red chilies, sliced
- 1 inch ginger root, peeled and sliced
- 1 teaspoon salt

Prepare **spice paste** by grinding or blending all ingredients together. Combine in a saucepan with all other ingredients and simmer until the pork is tender. If the gravy threatens to dry out before the pork is cooked, add a little more warm water.

TINARANSAY

In Northern Manado, where many of the population are Christian, the Muslim strictures on the eating of pork do not exist. 🕐🕐

- $1^1/_4$ pounds boneless pork shoulder or leg
- $2^1/_2$ inches ginger root, peeled and sliced
- 12 red chilies, seeded and sliced
- 3 shallots, peeled and sliced
- 2 tablespoons oil
- 5 kaffir lime leaves
- 2 turmeric leaves (optional)
- 3 stalks lemongrass, bruised and sliced
- 1 large ripe tomato, cut in wedges (optional)
- Salt to taste

Cut pork into 1-inch cubes. Grind or blend ginger, chilies and shallots coarsely.

Heat oil in wok or heavy saucepan and sauté the ground mixture for 2–3 minutes, until it changes color. Add pork and all remaining ingredients and continue sautéing over high heat, stirring, for 2 minutes.

Reduce heat, cover the wok or pan and cook the pork in its own juices until tender. If the meat threatens to dry out, add a little water from time to time.

Opposite:
Babi Masak Tomat (bottom) and Tinaransay (top).

RENDANG SAPI & KALIO HATI
Beef in Coconut Milk & Beef Liver in Coconut Milk

RENDANG SAPI

This is one of the most popular Padang dishes from West Sumatra. ⏱⏱

2 pounds top round beef
8 cups coconut milk (made from 2 coconuts if using freshly grated coconut)
3 *salam* leaves
3 kaffir lime leaves
3 fresh turmeric leaves (optional)
3 inches cinnamon stick
5 whole star anise
5 cardamom pods, bruised
1 teaspoon salt

Spice Paste:

8 red chilies, sliced
12 shallots, peeled and sliced
10 cloves garlic, peeled and sliced
2 inches ginger root, peeled and sliced
2 inches galangal (*laos*), peeled and sliced
1 teaspoon black peppercorns, crushed

Opposite:
*Rendang Sapi.
Kalio Hati not
shown.*

Prepare the **spice paste** by grinding or blending all ingredients finely.

Cut the beef into 1/4-inch-thick slices about 1-inch square. Put the beef, spice paste and all other ingredients into a wok and bring slowly to a boil, stirring constantly to prevent the coconut milk from separating. Cook over low heat, stirring from time to time, until the meat is very tender and all the sauce has evaporated. Continue cooking the beef, which will fry in the oil that has come out of the coconut milk, until rich brown.

KALIO HATI ⏱⏱

1 1/4 pounds beef liver, well trimmed, sliced and cut in 3/4-inch squares
3 cups coconut milk
1 teaspoon salt

Spice Paste:

8 shallots, peeled and sliced
3 cloves garlic, peeled and sliced
14 bird's eye chilies, sliced
1/2 inch galangal (*laos*), peeled and sliced
1/2 inch fresh turmeric, peeled and sliced
1/2 inch ginger root, peeled and sliced
2 tablespoons oil
1 stalk lemongrass, bruised
2 kaffir lime leaves

Prepare the **spice paste** by grinding all ingredients except oil, lemongrass and lime leaves. Heat oil in a wok and fry the ground mixture together with lemongrass and lime leaves for 2–3 minutes.

Add the liver and sauté for 2 minutes. Add the coconut milk and salt and simmer, uncovered, until the liver is tender and the sauce has thickened.

HAGAPE DAGING

Spiced Beef with Coconut

A coconut-rich beef dish from Ambon, in the Spice Islands or Maluku. Unlike some dishes with plenty of gravy, the meat is gently simmered until coated by only a little thick sauce. ⏱ ⏱

2 pounds beef top round
1 cup freshly grated or dried unsweetened coconut
2¹/₂ cups coconut milk
1 stalk lemongrass, bruised

Spice Paste:

¹/₄ teaspoon ground white pepper
2 inches galangal (*laos*), peeled and sliced
6 candlenuts
3 inches fresh turmeric, peeled and sliced (or 3 teaspoons powder)
3 inches ginger root, peeled and sliced
1 teaspoon salt
¹/₂ teaspoon coriander seeds
¹/₂ teaspoon cumin seeds
4 tablespoons oil

Opposite:
Hagape Daging (bottom) and Nasi Jagung (top). Recipe for Nasi Jagung on page 62.

Cut the beef into cubes of about ³/₄ inch. Gently fry the coconut in a dry wok, stirring constantly, until golden brown, then grind or blend until the oil begins to come out.

Prepare the **spice paste** by grinding or blending all ingredients, except the oil. Heat oil in a wok and sauté the spice paste until fragrant, then add the ground coconut, coconut milk, lemongrass and beef. Simmer, uncovered, until the beef is tender and the sauce is almost dry. If the sauce threatens to dry up completely before the meat is cooked, add a little hot water.

Helpful hint: As this is a rather dry dish, it should be accompanied by at least one other dish with plenty of liquid.

LAPIS MANADO
Seasoned Fried Beef Slices

As the name of this dish implies, it comes from Manado, in Northern Sulawesi. 🕐🕐

1½ pounds top round beef, in 1 piece
3 cloves
¼ teaspoon freshly grated nutmeg
1 teaspoon salt
6 cups water
Oil for deep frying

Spice Paste:

10 red chilies, seeded and chopped
1 inch ginger root, peeled and sliced
1 inch fresh turmeric, peeled and sliced
  (or 1 teaspoon powder)
1 inch *kencur*, peeled and sliced
2 teaspoons coriander seeds, crushed
1 teaspoon white peppercorns, crushed

Put the beef, cloves, nutmeg, salt and water in a large pan. Simmer, uncovered, until the beef is half cooked. Drain, reserving stock, and when the beef is cool enough to handle, cut into thin slices about 3 inches x 1½ inches.

While beef is cooking, prepare the **spice paste** by grinding or blending all ingredients finely. Put beef slices and spice paste in a pan with the reserved stock and simmer, uncovered, until the beef is tender and the gravy thickened. If stock has not been reduced to a thick gravy by the time the meat is tender, remove beef and continue simmering stock until thickened.

Drain beef, dry well, and deep fry in hot oil. Pour sauce over the beef and serve.

ES CAMPUR, ES APOKAT & ES KOLAK

Mixed Ice, Avocado Shake & Fruit in Coconut Milk

Indonesia has a multitude of thirst-quenching snacks that can be enjoyed as desserts. Known as *es* (ice), the contents depend upon availability and preference. Here are some typical recipes.

ES CAMPUR ⏱

$1/4$ ripe papaya, peeled and diced
$1/2$ avocado, peeled and diced
1 tomato, diced
$1/4$ ripe pineapple, peeled and diced
8 tablespoons agar-agar jelly cubes or flavored gelatin cubes
8 tablespoons diced fermented tapioca (*tape*), (optional)
8 tablespoons diced *kolang kaling* (palm fruit, available in cans)
1 young coconut, flesh removed with spoon (optional)
1 cup coconut water from the young coconut
$1/2$ cup condensed milk
$1/2$ cup palm sugar syrup (page 37)
4 cups crushed ice

Cut all fruits into tiny dice ($1/4$ inch). Combine with all other ingredients, except ice, and mix well. Add crushed ice and serve immediately.

ES APOKAT ⏱

4 ripe avocados, halved and flesh removed
$1/2$ cup palm sugar syrup (page 37)
4 tablespoons condensed milk
1 tablespoon lime juice
3 cups ice cubes

Combine avocado flesh with all other ingredients and puree in a blender until smooth.

ES KOLAK ⏱

4 cups coconut milk
4 tablespoons palm sugar syrup (page 37)
Pinch of salt
1 large or 2 small bananas, sliced
2 pieces of ripe jackfruit, finely diced
1 small sweet potato, peeled, diced, simmered until soft

Combine coconut milk, palm sugar and salt, then add all remaining ingredients Add a few ice cubes and serve.

KUE NAGASARI & PISANG GORENG
Steamed Banana Cakes & Fried Banana Cakes

KUE NAGASARI

Bananas are the most widely available fruit through-out Indonesia, so it's not surprising that they appear in so many desserts and cakes. 🕐🕐

- **1$\frac{1}{2}$ cups mung pea flour (*tepong hoen kwe*) or rice flour**
- **$\frac{1}{3}$ cup white sugar**
- **2$\frac{1}{4}$ cups coconut milk**
- **Pinch of salt**
- **6-inch squares of banana leaf**
- **6 small or 2 large bananas, cut in $\frac{1}{2}$-inch-thick slices about 2$\frac{1}{2}$ inches in length**

Combine the flour and sugar in a bowl and stir in coconut milk, mixing well. Add salt and slowly bring the mixture to a boil in a heavy pan (preferably non-stick). Simmer until the mixture is very thick, then leave to cool.

Put 1 heaped tablespoon of the mixture onto a square of banana leaf. Top with a piece of banana and cover with another tablespoonful of mixture. Wrap up the banana leaf, tucking in the sides first and then rolling it over envelope style. Steam for about 20 minutes, cool and serve at room temperature.

Helpful hints: Tepong Hoen Kwe is sold in paper-wrapped cylinders; sometimes, the flour is colored pink or green and the paper wrapper correspond-ingly colored. This flour gives a more delicate tex-ture than rice flour, although the latter is an accep-table substitute often used in Indonesia.

PISANG GORENG

Whole bananas dipped in batter and deep fried are very popular; if the bananas become over-ripe, they are often mashed and prepared by the following method. 🕐

- **6 medium-sized ripe bananas, peeled**
- **1 tablespoon white sugar**
- **1 tablespoon white flour**
- **Oil for deep frying**

Mash bananas finely and mix with sugar and white flour. Heat oil in a wok and drop in a large spoon-ful of batter. Cook several at one time, but do not overcrowd the wok or the temperature of the oil will be lowered. When cakes are crisp and golden brown, drain on paper towel and serve while still warm.

Opposite:
Kue Nagasari (bottom) and Pisang Goreng (top).

BUBUR SUMSUM & ONGOL-ONGOL
Rice Flour Dessert & Sago Flour Roll

BUBUR SUMSUM

Various types of flour made from sago, tapioca, rice and small round green mung peas are widely used for making simple desserts and cakes. Bubur Sumsum is the Indonesian equivalent of a Jewish mother's chicken soup: if you've a problem, eat a bowl of Bubur Sumsum and all will be well. ⏱

Opposite:
*Bubur Sumsum
(bottom) and
Ongol-Ongol (top).*

1$\frac{1}{2}$ cups rice flour
6 cups water
1 teaspoon powdered white writing chalk
Freshly grated coconut or moistened dried
   unsweetened coconut
$\frac{1}{2}$ teaspoon salt
Palm sugar syrup (page 37)

Combine flour, water and chalk and mix well. Strain through a fine sieve into a heavy pan, preferably nonstick. Bring to a boil, reduce heat and simmer for about 30 minutes until the mixture thickens.

Cool to room temperature and serve topped with freshly grated coconut mixed with salt, and pour over palm sugar syrup.

Helpful hint: The sort of chalk used for writing on blackboards may seem a surprising ingredient, but according to Indonesian cooks, it "adds a gentle, soft flavor."

ONGOL-ONGOL

An inexpensive dessert in Indonesia, where sago flour, palm sugar and coconut are always readily available. ⏱⏱

1 cup sago flour
1 cup chopped palm sugar
2 pandan leaves
3$\frac{1}{2}$ cups water
Large square of banana leaf or parchment
   paper
Freshly grated coconut or moistened dried
   unsweetened coconut
$\frac{1}{2}$ teaspoon salt
Palm sugar syrup (page 37)

Combine flour, sugar, pandan leaves and water in a heavy pan and bring to a boil. Simmer over low heat for 30 minutes until thickened, then leave until cool enough to handle.

Place the mixture on a large square of banana leaf and roll up in a cylinder. Fasten the ends with toothpicks and allow to cool. Serve the Ongol-Ongol sliced, sprinkled with a little coconut mixed with salt, and pour over palm sugar syrup.

Mail-order Sources of Ingredients

The ingredients used in this book can all be found in markets featuring the foods of Southeast Asia. Many of them can also be found in any well-stocked supermarket. Ingredients not found locally may be available from the mail-order markets listed below.

Anzen Importers
736 NE Union Ave.
Portland, OR 97232
Tel: 503-233-5111

Central Market
40th & Lamar St.
Austin, Texas
Tel: 512-206-1000

Dekalb World Farmers Market
3000 East Ponce De Leon
Decatur, GA 30034
Tel: 404-377-6401

Dean & Deluca
560 Broadway
New York, NY 10012
Tel: 800-221-7714 (outside NY);
800-431-1691 (in NY)

Gourmail, Inc.
816 Newton Road
Berwyn, PA 19312
Tel: 215-296-4620

House of Spices
76-17 Broadway
Jackson Heights
Queens, NY 11373
Tel: 718-507-4900

Kam Man Food Products
200 Canal Street
New York, NY 10013
Tel: 212-755-3566

Nancy's Specialty Market
P.O. Box 327
Wye Mills, MD 21679
Tel: 800-462-6291

Oriental Food Market and Cooking School
2801 Howard St.
Chicago, IL 60645
Tel: 312-274-2826

Oriental Market
502 Pampas Drive
Austin, TX 78752
Tel: 512-453-9058

Pacific Mercantile Company, Inc.
1925 Lawrence St.
Denver, CO 80202
Tel: 303-295-0293

Penn Herbs
603 North 2nd St.
Philadelphia, PA 19123
Tel: 800-523-9971

Rafal Spice Company
2521 Russell
Detroit, MI 48207
Tel: 313-259-6373

Siam Grocery
2745 Broadway
New York, NY 10025
Tel: 212-245-4660

Spice House
1048 N. Old World 3rd St.
Milwaukee, WI
Tel: 414-272-0977

Thailand Food Corp.
4821 N. Broadway St.
Chicago, IL 60640
Tel: 312-728-1199

Uwajimaya
PO Box 3003
Seattle, WA 98114
Tel: 206-624-6248

Vietnam Imports
922 W. Broad Street
Falls Church, VA 22046
Tel: 703-534-9441

Index